DIRECTOR MANUAL
Mission Control

Group
Loveland, Colorado

Mission Control Director Manual

Copyright © 1998 Group Publishing, Inc.

Credits
Space Mission Bible Camp Coordinator: Jody Brolsma
Chief Creative Officer: Joani Schultz
Copy Editor: Debbie Gowensmith
Art Director: Kari K. Monson
Cover Art Director: Lisa Chandler
Cover Photographer: Jafe Parsons
Illustrators: Dana Regan and Drew Rose
Production Manager: Gingar Kunkel

ISBN 0-7644-9809-6
Printed in the United States of America.
10 9 8 7 6 5 4 3 2 1   98 99

CONTENTS

Get Ready to Blast Off!

Space Mission Bible Camp Basics

Operation Kid-to-Kid™

Planning Your Space Mission Bible Camp

Recruitment

Leader Training

Publicity

Registration

Spaceship Tips
Secrets for a Successful Space Mission...........................149

Returning to Earth
Closing Program and Follow-Up Ideas..........................161

Index 177

Get Ready to Blast Off!

An Introduction to

Welcome to Space Mission Bible Camp!

Three...two...one...blast off! We're glad you've chosen to fly with us at Group's Space Mission Bible Camp! If you haven't used Group's VBS materials before, you're in for a real treat. Space Mission Bible Camp is an exciting, fun-filled, Bible-based program your kids will love. (We know because we tested everything in a pilot program last summer. Look for our Pilot Program Pointers to learn what we discovered and how that will make your program a blast!) Your teachers will love Space Mission Bible Camp, too, because it's so easy to prepare for! And *you'll* love it because kids will carry out a mission of God's love in ways they'll never forget.

Spaceship Tip

As Mission Control Director, you'll want to know what's happening each day. Refer to the "Space Mission Bible Camp Overview Chart" on pages 10-11 to get an overview of the Bible stories and biblical truths elementary kids cover. You'll discover how these truths will be reinforced creatively throughout each day.

Each day at Space Mission Bible Camp is packed with activities designed to launch kids on a mission of God's love. Kids start off each day by forming small groups called Flight Crews. All the Flight Crews gather at Sing & Play Blast Off to do fun motions to upbeat Bible songs that introduce kids to the concepts they'll be learning that day. Then Flight Crews "blast off" to five different Training Stations. They meet Chadder Chipmunk™ on video, play Have-a-Blast Games, sample marvelous Mission Munchies, explore the excitement and drama of Bible adventures, and create spectacular Space Crafts. Then crews gather together to participate in each day's Mission Send-Off Show Time. And throughout the week, children work on their own special mission—Operation Kid-to-Kid™—that allows them to impact kids around the globe!

Preschoolers have a special Space Mission Bible Camp program of their own. They join the older kids for opening and closing activities each day, and in between they enjoy fun, age-appropriate, Bible-learning activities in the Preschool Bible SpacePlace. Each day there, preschoolers hear a fun Bible story and then explore the story with all five senses through Blast Off Discovery Stations. Later, children continue their discoveries and work off some energy during their outdoor Spaceport Playtime. They also get to meet Chadder Chipmunk and enjoy Mission Munchies made by the older kids. One day, they'll even make the snacks for the entire Space Mission Bible Camp! The Preschool Bible SpacePlace Director Manual contains complete instructions for setting up, organizing, and running the Preschool Bible SpacePlace.

This Mission Control Director Manual is your guide to launching a successful Space Mission Bible Camp. It contains everything you need to plan a successful program, recruit and train volunteers, publicize your program, and follow up with kids and their families after Space Mission Bible Camp. **The countdown has begun! Get ready to launch your kids on a mission of God's love they'll never forget!**

SPACE MISSION BIBLE CAMP OVERVIEW CHART

This is what everyone else is doing! At Space Mission Bible Camp, the daily Bible Point is carefully integrated into each Training Station activity to reinforce Bible learning. Each station is an important part of kids' overall learning experience.

	BIBLE POINT	BIBLE STORY	BIBLE VERSE	SING & PLAY BLAST OFF	SPACE CRAFTS	HAVE-A-BLAST GAMES
DAY 1	God helps us to be kind.	Joseph shows kindness to his brothers (Genesis 37–45; 50:15-21).	"Be kind and compassionate to one another, forgiving each other, just as in Christ God forgave you" (Ephesians 4:32).	● I Can Do All Things ● This Is My Commandment ● Be Kind to One Another ● Little Bit of Love (chorus and verse 1)	**Craft** Tube-a-loon™ Rockets **Application** In order to fly, the Tube-a-loon Rocket needs to be filled with air. We need to be filled with kindness so we can carry out our mission of God's love.	**Games** ● Kindness Cliques ● Moonwalk ● Spacesuit Stuffing ● Joseph and His Brothers ● Color Catch **Application** With God's help, we can be kind, which draws us together and builds others up.
DAY 2	God helps us to be thankful.	Hannah praises God for Samuel (1 Samuel 1–2:10).	"Give thanks to the Lord, for he is good; his love endures forever" (Psalm 107:1).	● Everybody Give Thanks! ● Little Bit of Love (add verse 2) ● He Can Do ● Lord, Put a Smile, Smile, Smile on My Face	**Craft** Thankfulness Bracelets **Application** The glow-in-the-dark Thankfulness Bracelets remind us that we can thank God any time and anywhere. *(Kids will also be introduced to Operation Kid-to-Kid™ and will work in their Flight Crews to decide who will bring each item.)*	**Games** ● Puno Hvala! Terima Kasih! Gracias! ● Thanksgiving Pass-Along ● Set Free! ● Overflowing Blessings ● Everybody Give Thanks ● Hannah's Hot Seat **Application** God has given us lots of things to be thankful for!
DAY 3	God helps us to be helpful.	A little boy shares his lunch, and Jesus feeds five thousand (John 6:1-14).	"Serve one another in love" (Galatians 5:13b).	● Great Is the Lord ● I Will Praise You ● Down in My Heart ● Little Bit of Love (add verse 3)	**Craft** Blast Off Rockets **Application** Jesus took a little boy's lunch and made it go a long, long way. Our Blast Off Rockets use just a little rocket fuel to launch a long way, too!	**Games** ● Rocket Launch ● Moon-Rock Relay ● The Impossible Loop Pass ● Belly Laughs ● Superbat **Application** God can do anything! Even when we're only able to help a little, God does amazing things with what we give.
DAY 4	God helps us to believe in Jesus.	Thomas believes in Jesus (John 19:17–20:29).	"Believe in the Lord Jesus, and you will be saved" (Acts 16:31b).	● We Must Believe ● Little Bit of Love (add verse 4) ● I Believe in Jesus ● J. E. S. U. S.	**Craft** Walkie-Talkies **Application** Thomas had a hard time believing that Jesus rose from the dead. People won't believe the amazing thing that these Walkie-Talkies can do!	**Games** ● Launch Pad ● Toe-Ticklin' Tombstone Trek ● Space Spinners ● Thomas' Troubles **Application** We can celebrate because Jesus died and rose again.
DAY 5	God helps us to be faithful.	Paul and Silas praise God in jail (Acts 16:16-34).	"Trust in the Lord with all your heart and lean not on your own understanding" (Proverbs 3:5).	● Great Is the Lord ● I Can Do All Things ● Little Bit of Love (entire song)	**Craft** Operation Kid-to-Kid school packs **Application** Paul and Silas were faithful when they shared God's love with the jailer. Operation Kid-to-Kid is a way to faithfully carry out our mission of God's love.	**Games** ● Moon Rover ● Pass It On ● Smugglers ● Spread-the-Word Soccer **Application** God helps us faithfully share the good news of his love.

This overview chart shows you the entire program at a glance. Refer to the chart to see how each Training Station's activities supplement other activities to help launch kids on a mission of God's love.

MISSION MUNCHIES	CHADDER'S SPACE MISSION THEATER	BIBLE EXPLORATION	MISSION SEND-OFF SHOW TIME
Snack Joseph's Kindness Cups **Application** Joseph was kind to his brothers even though they threw him in a dark pit. God helps us to be kind, too.	**Video Segment** Chadder Chipmunk™ goes to Space Mission Bible Camp to learn about space travel, but a mean Exterminator thinks he's a pesky rodent and is out to get him. Nikki, a camp counselor, helps Chadder understand that God helps us treat everyone with kindness. **Application** ● When someone treats you unkindly, how do you feel about that person? ● How does God help you to be kind? ● Draw a picture of yourself inside the rocket on your "Bible Blast Off" poster to show that you're launching a mission of God's love.	**Joseph** ● Get "tossed" into a "pit," and listen as Joseph's brothers sell him to a caravan of travelers. ● Stand up and crouch down as they learn about the ups and downs of Joseph's life. ● Sit in the pit, and talk about how we can be kind even when life is the "pits."	● Listen to reports on how others carried out their mission of kindness at Space Mission Bible Camp. ● Meet "Billy," a special friend, and reach out to him with love and kindness. ● Experience what it might be like to go without something; then learn a little bit about Operation Kid-to-Kid.
Snack Hannah's Happy Smiles **Application** Hannah thanked and praised God when God answered her prayers and gave her a baby.	**Video Segment** Chadder meets Dr. Davidson, a top NASA engineer, who finds out that she didn't get a grant for research. In spite of her disappointment, Dr. Davidson tells Chadder that she has many other things to be thankful for. Jake Armstrong, a former astronaut, rescues Chadder from the Exterminator. **Application** ● What are you thankful for? ● When should we give thanks? ● Why do we sometimes forget to say, "Thank you"?	**Hannah** ● Hear an argument between Hannah and Peninnah to discover why Hannah was so sad. ● Hold out their arms to understand how Hannah's arms ached for a baby. ● Explore ways to show that we're thankful people.	● Listen to reports on how others carried out their mission of thankfulness at Space Mission Bible Camp. ● Go in pairs on a mission of thankfulness. ● Pass streamers, and tell things they're thankful for. Then use the streamers to celebrate all the great things God has given them.
Snack Helping Hands **Application** A little boy helped by sharing his lunch with Jesus. God helps us "lend a hand," too!	**Video Segment** As Chadder runs from the Exterminator, he meets Emma, a homeless woman who shares her sunflower seeds with him. Chadder discovers that being helpful in small ways is just as important as being helpful in big ways. Later, Jake helps Brian and Lisa on their troublesome science projects by suggesting that they work together rather than compete against each other. **Application** ● How do you feel when someone helps you? ● How have you helped others? ● What's one way you can help someone this week?	**Feeding the Five Thousand** ● Try to feed themselves without bending their arms. Discover that they must feed each other to accomplish their task. ● Meet the disciple Andrew, and hear how Jesus fed a huge crowd with a boy's tiny lunch.	● Listen to reports on how others carried out their mission of helpfulness at Space Mission Bible Camp. ● Share one dinner roll among the entire group. ● Help crew members stand as they share ways they can be helpful.
Snack Believin' Butterflies **Application** If we believe that Jesus died for our sins, we can have new life.	**Video Segment** Brian and Lisa are ready to try their new, improved science project, but Brian is afraid it'll be a failure. Dr. Davidson reminds Brian that Thomas thought Jesus was a failure when Jesus died. Jesus proved that he was victorious when he conquered death and rose from the dead. Chadder decides to rely on Jesus to solve his troubles with the Exterminator. **Application** ● Why is it hard to believe in Jesus? ● How can we let others know we believe in Jesus? ● How can you help others believe in Jesus?	**Thomas Doubts Jesus' Resurrection** ● Eavesdrop on the disciples when Jesus appears after his death. ● Hunt for plastic eggs that contain special clues about Jesus' death. ● Meet the disciple Thomas, and try to convince him that Jesus really is alive. ● Learn how to say, "I believe in Jesus" in sign language.	● Listen to reports on how others carried out their mission of believing in Jesus at Space Mission Bible Camp. ● Watch as crew leaders stain "Jesus' robe"; then sing "We Must Believe." After the song, the robe will be pure white again! ● Hear Thomas tell that he believes in Jesus.
Snack Jail Cell Snackers **Application** Paul and Silas showed their faithfulness in prison by singing and praying. Their faithfulness helped the jailer believe in Jesus.	**Video Segment** The Exterminator captures Chadder and ties him to a rocket that's attached to the shuttle. As the Exterminator leaves, she gets caught on a giant hook. Jake conquers his fears and rescues Chadder...then they both rescue the Exterminator! Chadder and the Exterminator become friends, and everyone celebrates Dr. Davidson's exciting new job at a lab in space. **Application** ● When is it hard for you to be faithful? ● Why do you think God wants us to be faithful? ● How can you be faithful this week?	**Paul and Silas** ● Get "thrown" in jail, and think about how dark, smelly, and uncomfortable it might have been for Paul and Silas. ● Sing a praise song in jail, and experience an "earthquake."	● Listen to reports on how others carried out their mission of faithfulness at Space Mission Bible Camp. ● Present their Operation Kid-to-Kid school packs as an offering to God. ● Review the Bible stories and daily Bible Points. ● Autograph crew members' "Bible Blast Off" posters.

Inspecting Your
◉ Space Mission Bible Camp ◉
Starter Kit

Before you launch your Space Mission Bible Camp program, inspect your Starter Kit to make sure it contains all the following items:

○ **Mission Control Director Manual (you're reading it now!)**—This is your guide to running Space Mission Bible Camp. It includes everything you need to plan, staff, and promote your church's best program ever! In it you'll find photocopiable handouts, letters, certificates, and more.

○ *Countdown!* **video**—This video provides an overview of the entire Space Mission Bible Camp program. As you watch the video, you'll meet teachers and kids who've participated in Space Mission Bible Camp. You'll see for yourself how much fun Bible learning can be. The video also contains training material so you can feel confident that your staff is well-prepared to run its very own Space Mission Bible Camp. Additionally, your Mission Control Director Manual tells you how to use this video as a quick promotional tool to get your church, kids, parents, and teachers excited about your program.

○ **Preschool Bible SpacePlace Director Manual**—This guide outlines five days of complete programs for children between the ages of three and five. The manual also contains supply lists, room setup and decoration ideas, exciting Bible-teaching ideas, and more to make your Preschool Bible SpacePlace *the* place to be!

○ **seven Training Station leader manuals:**
  ● **Sing & Play Blast Off Leader Manual**
  ● **Mission Munchies Leader Manual**
  ● **Space Crafts Leader Manual**
  ● **Bible Exploration Leader Manual**
  ● **Chadder's Space Mission Theater Leader Manual***
  ● **Have-a-Blast Games Leader Manual**
  ● **Mission Send-Off Show Time Leader Manual**

Each leader manual introduction contains detailed instructions for before, during, and after Space Mission Bible Camp, plus an overview of the entire program. Leader manuals include clear, step-by-step directions for each activity, guided discussion questions, Spaceship Tips, and Pilot Program Pointers to make sure everything goes smoothly.

*Requires *Chadder's Space Mission Adventure* video (available from Group Publishing, Inc., and your local Christian bookstore).

○ **Sing & Play Blast Off audiocassette**—This audiocassette provides Bible songs your kids will love, including the Space Mission Bible Camp theme song, "Little Bit of Love." The cassette is recorded in split-track format so you can use just the accompaniment or can add kids' voices. After you've listened to the cassette, give it to your Sing & Play Blast Off Leader. He or she will use the cassette to teach kids the Space Mission Bible Camp songs. You may want to order additional cassettes so other leaders (especially those for Space Crafts, Mission Munchies, and Have-a-Blast Games) can play the songs in the background as kids visit their Training Stations.

○ **Space Mission Bible Camp Drama & Sound Effects audiocassette**—This audiocassette of music, dramatic scripts, and sound effects will add fun and excitement to your Sing & Play Blast Off, Bible Exploration, and Mission Send-Off Show Time. (Check out the GaWheezer-9 scripts on side 1. Kids will get a kick out of this lovable robot friend!)

○ **Operation Kid-to-Kid packet**—On Day 2, kids will learn about an exciting, meaningful mission project called Operation Kid-to-Kid. This packet explains what Operation Kid-to-Kid is, how it was developed, who it will impact, and how the kids at your VBS will carry it out.

○ **Elementary Student Book**—This book contains elementary students' five Mission Logbooks, an Operation Kid-to-Kid newsletter and mission-item selection sheet, an eleven-by-thirty-seven-inch foldout "Bible Blast Off" poster, plus a bonus game that will help kids remember Bible truths long after Space Mission Bible Camp.

○ **Preschool Student Book**—This book contains preschoolers' five Mission Logbooks (complete with Bible activity pages), an Operation Kid-to-Kid newsletter and mission-item selection sheet, an eleven-by-thirty-seven-inch foldout "Bible Blast Off" poster especially for preschoolers, and a matching game to reinforce Bible learning at home.

○ **sample Talkie Tapes™ strip**—This amazing strip of plastic actually talks! Just follow the instructions on the attached sheet to hear the Talkie Tapes strip say, "Jesus loves you!" Kids use Talkie Tapes strips to create a spectacular Space Craft they'll play with again and again.

○ **sample Blast Off Rocket Kit**—This highflying craft will amaze kids and will remind them of the big impact they can have. Follow the instructions on the enclosed sheet to create and launch your own Blast Off Rocket.

○ **"Training Station Signs and Bonus Planning" poster**—Count down to Space Mission Bible Camp fun using the planning calendar on the back of this poster. Hang the calendar in your office or another prominent place to remind you of key dates in your Space Mission Bible Camp planning. When it's time to blast off, photocopy the arrows to help direct kids to their Training Stations. Cut apart the colorful Training Station signs, and post them on doors or in hallways.

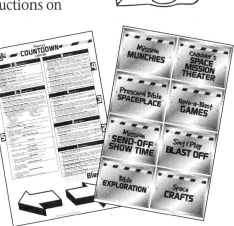

13

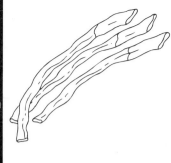

○ **Brite-Tites™**—Kids will use this nylon hosiery in Bible Exploration, Have-a-Blast Games, and Preschool Bible SpacePlace.

○ **sample Home Mission Activity Panel**—Help family members grow closer as they carry out their mission of God's love using the easy ideas hidden behind the windows on this "mission control board." Plus the back of the board is filled with even more innovative ideas to encourage family "together time."

○ **bag of sample items**—Add dazzle to your program with these "extras." In this bag you'll find publicity helps to build excitement about your program, awards to recognize everyone's contribution, and souvenirs to leave a lasting impression.

If any Starter Kit items are missing or damaged, contact your local Christian bookstore for prompt replacement.

If you checked off everything on this list, you're ready to launch your program.

May God bless you as you plan your
Space Mission Bible Camp program!

Space Mission Bible Camp Basics

What You'll Want to Know

Before You Blast Off

Why Space Mission Bible Camp?

What makes Group's Space Mission Bible Camp different from other VBS programs?

● **At Space Mission Bible Camp, kids learn one important Bible Point each day.** Instead of trying to teach kids more than they can remember or apply, Space Mission Bible Camp focuses on one key biblical concept: **God helps us.** This Bible Point is reinforced daily through Bible stories, Bible verses, and hands-on activities that help kids discover the strength God gives them. Kids who attend your church regularly will enjoy discovering this important truth in fresh, new ways. And neighborhood kids who come to your VBS will hear the "meat" of the gospel right away. Each day kids will learn something new about how God helps them carry out a mission of his love.

Day 1: God helps us to be kind.
Day 2: God helps us to be thankful.
Day 3: God helps us to be helpful.
Day 4: God helps us to believe in Jesus.
Day 5: God helps us to be faithful.

● **At Space Mission Bible Camp, kids learn the way they learn best.** Not all kids learn the same way, so Space Mission Bible Camp offers seven daily Training Stations to meet the needs of all kinds of learners. Each child will come away from each day remembering the Bible Point because kids will pick it up in a way that matches their learning style.

Spaceship Tip

To help little ones learn more easily, preschoolers will learn the Bible Point for Day 5 as "God helps us to be faithful followers."

 **Sing & Play Blast Off's** songs and motions will teach the Bible Point to your **musical learners.**

Have-a-Blast Games, Bible Exploration, and Space Crafts allow **bodily-kinesthetic learners** to wiggle and move as they explore the Bible Point in active ways.

  Chadder's Space Mission Theater lets **visual learners** discover the Bible Point through watching the *Chadder's Space Mission Adventure* video.

Mission Munchies allows **interpersonal learners** the opportunity to explore how God helps us as they make and serve snacks for the entire Space Mission Bible Camp.

17

Mission Send-Off Show Time's dramatic and interactive programs help **linguistic learners** remember each day's Bible Point.

Every Training Station asks meaningful, thought-provoking questions that encourage **logical and introspective learners** to think about and apply the Bible Point.

● **At Space Mission Bible Camp, teachers teach the way they teach best.** Just like kids, not all teachers think alike. Instead of forcing every teacher to teach the same material, Space Mission Bible Camp provides opportunities for you to enlist a variety of teachers. Got a great storyteller in your congregation? Recruit that person to lead Bible Exploration. Got a great athlete? Recruit that person to lead Have-a-Blast Games. Because each Training Station is different, teachers can volunteer in their areas of expertise. And volunteers who are intimidated by the idea of teaching can join your staff as Flight Crew Leaders.

● **At Space Mission Bible Camp, no activity stands alone.** Instead of leading independent, isolated classes, Training Station Leaders see all the kids each day. Sing & Play Blast Off songs play in the background during other activities. Space Crafts become game equipment for Have-a-Blast Games. The Have-a-Blast Games Leader serves as an assistant Mission Munchies chef. The Bible Exploration Leader and the Mission Send-Off Show Time Leader share supplies and volunteers. All Training Station Leaders assist in Mission Send-Off Show Time. Each member of your Space Mission Bible Camp staff provides a unique and important part of kids' total VBS experience. With everyone working together, your staff will soar through the week.

● **At Space Mission Bible Camp, kids take responsibility for what they're learning.** Throughout the week, kids travel to Training Stations with their Flight Crews—small groups of three to five kids. On the first day, each child chooses a job that he or she will do throughout the week. Kids may be Readers, Navigators, Materials Managers, Cheerleaders, or Prayer People. From time to time, Training Station Leaders will call on kids to complete tasks that are part of their job descriptions.

Each Flight Crew also has an adult or teenage Flight Crew Leader. Flight Crew Leaders aren't teachers. They're simply part of Flight Crew families—like older brothers or sisters. Flight Crew Leaders participate in all the activities and encourage kids to talk about and apply what they're learning. Crew leaders who participated in Space Mission Bible Camp pilot programs saw kids encouraging other kids during the activities, helping younger crew members with difficult tasks, and reminding each other to use kind words. At Space Mission Bible Camp, kids put God's love into action!

● **At Space Mission Bible Camp, everyone is treated with respect.** Because kids travel in combined-age Flight Crews, big kids and little kids learn to work together. Instead of trying to compete with children their own age, older children help younger children during Space Crafts and Have-a-Blast Games. Younger children spark older children's imaginations during Bible Exploration and Mission Send-Off Show Time.

Pilot Program Pointer

"The older kids at my church like being with their friends. They'll complain if they have to be with the 'little' kids." Many people are hesitant to try teaching combined-age groups because they're afraid kids will balk at something new. You can let kids partner with same-age friends if they're really reluctant. But at our pilot programs, we discovered that kids enjoyed being in combined-age Flight Crews. Sure, it was a little different at first, but as kids warmed up to their crew mates, we saw them working together, helping each other, and forming friendships. There were few complaints, and discipline problems were almost nonexistent.

Studies show that children learn as much—or more—when they're linked with kids of different ages. In fact, one study observed that children naturally chose to play with other children their age only 6 percent of the time. They played with children at least one year older or younger than them 55 percent of the time.

Think of Flight Crews as families in which kids naturally learn with and from one another. Social skills improve, self-esteem rises, cooperation increases, and discipline problems diminish.

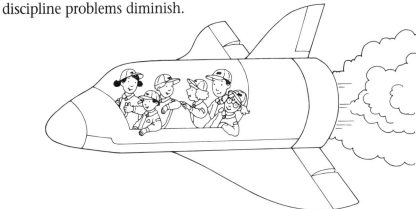

Combined-age Flight Crews also allow people of any age (even entire families) to join you for your Space Mission Bible Camp program. You can even use combined-age Flight Crews to teach kids about being part of the body of Christ!

Knowing and understanding these distinctives will help you present Space Mission Bible Camp to your church or committee.

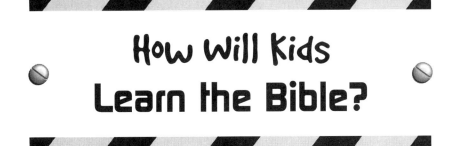

How Will Kids Learn the Bible?

Each day, kids will be exposed to a Bible Point as well as to a corresponding Bible story and verse. The chart on page 20 shows the Bible content kids will cover each day.

If you usually incorporate memory verses into your program, you can have kids memorize the daily Bible verses provided in this chart. Ideas to help kids learn these Bible verses are included in both the Elementary Student Book and the Preschool Student Book.

At each Training Station, kids will encounter a different presentation of the Bible Point, Bible story, or Bible verse.

Sing & Play Blast Off
● The Sing & Play Blast Off Leader repeats the Bible Point each day.
● In addition to fun praise songs, kids sing at least one song each day that specifically ties into that day's Bible Point. For example, on Day 4 children learn

Spaceship Tip

At each Training Station, kids will be carefully listening to hear the Bible Point so they can respond by shouting, "Blast off!" Watch their excitement and enthusiasm—and listening skills—build throughout the week!

Day	Bible Point	Bible Story	Bible Verse
DAY 1	God helps us to be kind.	Joseph shows kindness to his brothers (Genesis 37–45; 50:15-21).	"Be kind and compassionate to one another, forgiving each other, just as in Christ God forgave you" (Ephesians 4:32).
DAY 2	God helps us to be thankful.	Hannah praises God for Samuel (1 Samuel 1–2:10).	"Give thanks to the Lord, for he is good; his love endures forever" (Psalm 107:1).
DAY 3	God helps us to be helpful.	A little boy shares his lunch, and Jesus feeds five thousand (John 6:1-14).	"Serve one another in love" (Galatians 5:13b).
DAY 4	God helps us to believe in Jesus.	Thomas believes in Jesus (John 19:17–20:29).	"Believe in the Lord Jesus, and you will be saved" (Acts 16:31b).
DAY 5	God helps us to be faithful.	Paul and Silas praise God in jail (Acts 16:16-34).	"Trust in the Lord with all your heart and lean not on your own understanding" (Proverbs 3:5).

the song "We Must Believe" to go along with the Bible Point "God helps us to believe in Jesus."

● Each day kids learn a new verse of the Space Mission Bible Camp theme song, "Little Bit of Love." Each day's verse focuses on the corresponding daily Bible story.

● Each day the Sing & Play Blast Off Leader reads the daily Bible verse and summarizes the daily Bible story.

Space Crafts

● The Space Crafts Leader repeats the Bible Point each day.

● Kids make crafts that remind them of each day's Bible story, such as Thankfulness Bracelets (Day 2) and Blast Off Rockets (Day 3).

● Kids listen to the Sing & Play Blast Off songs as they're working.

● The Space Crafts Leader asks questions to help kids review and apply the Bible Point and the Bible story.

● Kids experience what it means to carry out a mission of God's love through Operation Kid-to-Kid.

Chadder's Space Mission Theater

● In each day's video segment, Chadder Chipmunk hears the daily Bible Point and the Bible story.

● The Chadder's Space Mission Theater Leader repeats the Bible Point each day.

● Kids apply Chadder's experiences to their own lives through role-play, problem-solving, and other short activities. Kids read the Bible verses to see how God helps them respond to life's difficulties.

Mission Munchies

- The Mission Munchies Leader repeats the Bible Point each day.
- Kids make and eat snacks that reinforce the daily Bible story, such as Joseph's Kindness Cups (Day 1) and Jail Cell Snackers (Day 5).
- Kids show God's love by serving others. Each day one set of Flight Crews makes the snacks for the entire VBS!
- Kids listen to Sing & Play Blast Off songs as they make and eat their snacks.

Have-a-Blast Games

- The Have-a-Blast Games Leader repeats the Bible Point each day.
- Kids play games that encourage them to apply what they've learned. For example, on Day 1 kids apply the Bible Point "God helps us to be kind" by saying kind words as they stuff a "spacesuit" with balloons during a game.
- Kids listen to Sing & Play Blast Off songs as they play games.
- The Have-a-Blast Games Leader connects each game to the daily Bible Point.

Bible Exploration

- The Bible Exploration Leader repeats the Bible Point each day.
- Kids experience the daily Bible story in a hands-on way. For example, on Day 4 kids meet Thomas and try to convince him that Jesus really rose from the dead.
- Kids discuss ways they can apply the daily Bible Point and Bible story to their lives. For example, on Day 3 they apply the Bible Point "God helps us to be helpful" by helping their crew members eat crackers.

Mission Send-Off Show Time

- The Mission Send-Off Show Time Leader repeats the Bible Point each day.
- Kids repeat the Sing & Play Blast Off songs they've learned that day.
- Kids use drama to apply what they've learned throughout the day. For example, on Day 1 they meet "Billy" and reach out to him with gentleness and kindness.

Preschool Bible SpacePlace

- Preschoolers sing the Sing & Play Blast Off songs with the older kids.
- The Preschool Bible SpacePlace Leader tells each day's Bible story in a fun, involving way.
- The Preschool Bible SpacePlace Director repeats the Bible Point during each Blast Off Discovery Station activity.
- Preschoolers hear the Bible story and the Bible Point as they watch *Chadder's Space Mission Adventure*.
- Preschoolers make and eat snacks that reinforce the daily Bible story.
- Preschoolers sing additional songs that reinforce the daily Bible Point or Bible story.
- Preschoolers participate in Mission Send-Off Show Time with the older kids.

As you can see, Space Mission Bible Camp is packed with Bible-based activities your kids will love!

What's a Training Station?

The Space Mission Bible Camp format is modeled after a space-and-science camp. At space-and-science camps, kids learn how astronauts train for space missions; then kids explore training stations such as a space shuttle simulator, a robotics lab, a model rocket-building lab, and a ropes course for physical training.

At Space Mission Bible Camp, kids blast into Bible learning as they visit various Training Stations each day. Each Training Station features a different space-camp-inspired, Bible-learning activity. Some stations—such as Sing & Play Blast Off, Mission Munchies, and Mission Send-Off Show Time—accommodate all the Space Mission Bible Camp "astronauts" simultaneously. Kids will visit other Training Stations in smaller groups.

Elementary-age kids visit the following Training Stations each day:
● Sing & Play Blast Off
● Space Crafts
● Have-a-Blast Games
● Mission Munchies
● Chadder's Space Mission Theater
● Bible Exploration
● Mission Send-Off Show Time

Preschoolers spend most of their time in the Preschool Bible SpacePlace, but they visit the following Training Stations each day:
● Sing & Play Blast Off
● Chadder's Space Mission Theater
● Mission Send-Off Show Time

Each Training Station is staffed by an adult leader. If you have more than 150 kids in your program, you may want to assign two adult leaders to each Training Station. They can team teach a large group of kids or can set up identical Training Stations for two smaller groups in separate areas.

If you have up to 150 kids, your church might be set up like this...

Spaceship Tip

On Day 1 only, preschoolers skip Sing & Play Blast Off and go straight to Preschool Bible SpacePlace. This allows little ones to meet their Space-Place Director, Flight Crew Leaders, and Flight Crew members. Plus, preschoolers get to make Mission Munchies on Day 1, and the extra time helps them accomplish this *big* task!

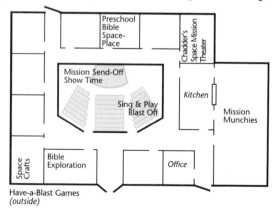

If you have more than 150 kids, your church might be set up like this...

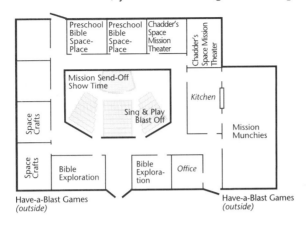

What's a Flight Crew?

When astronauts take part in a space mission, they work with a flight crew. During the space mission, each crew member has an important role in accomplishing the mission.

As you set up your Space Mission Bible Camp program, you'll assign kids to Flight Crews. On Day 1, kids will report to their Flight Crews right away, just as they would on a real space mission. Since Flight Crew members will work closely during the week, Flight Crews will encourage kids to make new friends at Space Mission Bible Camp. They'll also provide an organizational structure that will help kids progress from station to station in an orderly manner.

Flight Crews consist of three to five children and an adult or teenage Flight Crew Leader. If you're expecting visitors or want to encourage outreach, assign three children to each Flight Crew. Then encourage children to invite their friends

Spaceship Tip

Be sure to distribute the "For Flight Crew Leaders Only" handouts (pp. 111-116) to all crew leaders during your leader training time. Have extra handouts available at Space Mission Bible Camp for crew leaders who are unable to attend leader training.

to "fill up" their crews. If your attendance is pretty steady, assign up to five children to each crew. If possible, assign one child from each age level to each crew. "Your Flight Crew 'Family' " the developmental chart and illustration below, highlights the unique contribution children from each age level can make to a Flight Crew. The "Who's Who on the Crew?" chart on page 25 lists the five jobs Flight Crew members may fill during Space Mission Bible Camp.

Preschoolers' Flight Crews consist of up to five preschoolers and an adult or teenage crew leader.

Detailed instructions for setting up Flight Crews begin on page 135. Qualifications for crew leaders are listed on page 91.

Your Flight Crew "Family"

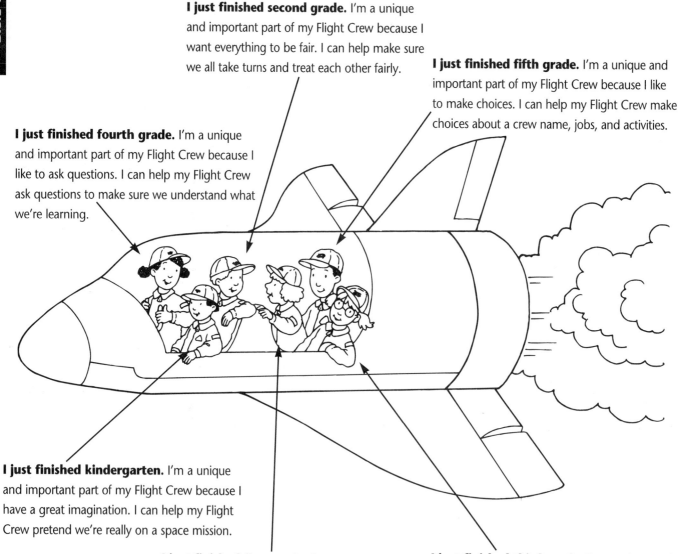

I just finished second grade. I'm a unique and important part of my Flight Crew because I want everything to be fair. I can help make sure we all take turns and treat each other fairly.

I just finished fifth grade. I'm a unique and important part of my Flight Crew because I like to make choices. I can help my Flight Crew make choices about a crew name, jobs, and activities.

I just finished fourth grade. I'm a unique and important part of my Flight Crew because I like to ask questions. I can help my Flight Crew ask questions to make sure we understand what we're learning.

I just finished kindergarten. I'm a unique and important part of my Flight Crew because I have a great imagination. I can help my Flight Crew pretend we're really on a space mission.

I just finished first grade. I'm a unique and important part of my Flight Crew because I like to be the best. I can help encourage my Flight Crew to be the best it can be.

I just finished third grade. I'm a unique and important part of my Flight Crew because I like to be challenged. I can help younger members of my Flight Crew with challenging projects.

24

Who's Who on the Crew?

During Sing & Play Blast Off on Day 1, kids will choose Flight Crew jobs and place job stickers (from Space Mission sticker sheets) on their name badges. You can expect each of the following jobs to be represented in each Flight Crew. If crews have fewer than five kids, some kids may have more than one job.

In addition to the five jobs listed below, each crew should have an adult or teenage crew leader. You can count on the crew leader to help kids complete the activities at each Training Station.

Kids are excited about having special jobs! Each leader manual suggests ways Training Station Leaders can call on kids to fulfill the job responsibilities they've chosen.

Jobs	Duties
Reader	• likes to read • reads Bible passages aloud
Navigator	• likes to help others • chooses action ideas for traveling between Training Stations (such as shuffling, skipping, hopping, galloping, or marching) • serves as line leader to guide crew through daily schedule
Materials Manager	• likes to pass out and collect supplies • passes out and collects Student Books • carries the crew's tote bag until the day is over
Cheerleader	• likes to smile and make people happy • makes sure people use kind words and actions • leads group in cheering during Have-a-Blast Games
Prayer Person	• likes to pray and isn't afraid to pray aloud • makes sure the group takes time to pray each day • leads or opens prayer times

Spaceship Tip

Each Flight Crew will need one tote bag in which to carry its Student Books, Space Mission sticker sheets Operation Kid-to-Kid items, and some of the crafts. Space Mission Bible Camp tote bags are available from Group Publishing and your local Christian bookstore.

Pilot Program Pointer

It's important that upper-elementary kids under-stand the specifics of their jobs. We discovered that assigning kids this age as "Floaters" who could fill in wherever there was a need gave them too much free-dom and not enough direc-tion. Our upper-elementary Floaters wandered around and complained about being bored. When we gave them specific roles, such as Assistant Chef or Assistant Space Crafts Leader, they did a super job of helping out!

Pilot Program Pointer

Make sure you choose more mature fifth- and sixth-graders for leadership roles. Many kids this age still enjoy being crew mem-bers and participating in all activities. In our pilot pro-gram, we assumed that one fifth-grade boy would make a great preschool crew leader. As it turned out, he felt slighted because he couldn't make his own cool craft or participate fully in other activities. Be sure to ask kids what they'd like to do instead of assuming they'd rather opt "out."

Where Do Fifth- and Sixth- Graders Fit In?

Many churches are unsure how to handle upper-elementary kids; they seem too old for some children's ministry programs and too young for youth group. With Space Mission Bible Camp, upper-elementary kids can fill a number of roles. Check out the following options to find the perfect fit for your fifth- and sixth-graders. They can...

● **join Flight Crews as Assistant Flight Crew Leaders.** Many upper-elementary kids are ready for simple leadership roles, but they still enjoy partici-pating in activities such as games, snack time, crafts, and biblical dramas. As Assistant Flight Crew Leaders, they can help their crew leaders by keeping kids together, working with younger children during Space Crafts, or doing the more difficult jobs during Mission Munchies service.

● **become Assistant Training Station Leaders.** Your fifth- and sixth-graders are developing their gifts and talents, discovering the things they excel at and enjoy. Being an Assistant Training Station Leader is a great way to encourage kids toward this discovery. Do you know an older child who's developing a love for drama and storytelling? Use him or her as an Assistant Mission Send-Off Show Time Leader or an Assistant Bible Exploration Leader. What about a child who enjoys sports and other athletic activities? Ask him or her to be an Assistant Have-a-Blast Games Leader. Your Training Station Leaders will love the extra help, and older kids will enjoy the added responsibility.

● **help with Preschool Bible SpacePlace registration.** Some fifth- and sixth-graders are nurturing and caring—great qualities for helping preschoolers find their way at Space Mission Bible Camp. For the first day or two, have a few upper-elementary kids available to help preschoolers find their Flight Crew Leaders, show preschoolers the restroom, or play with a shy child to get him or her accustomed to Preschool Bible SpacePlace.

● **create an upper-elementary Sing-Along Crew.** Older children (who might normally hesitate to sing and move to music) will enjoy teaching song motions and leading younger children in Sing & Play Blast Off. Ask a group of upper-elementary kids to work with the Sing & Play Blast Off Leader to learn the words and motions to all thirteen Space Mission Bible Camp songs. The Sing-Along Crew will add visual excitement and energy to your singing time.

Do Teenagers Have a Role at Space Mission Bible Camp?

Teenagers have an important role in making Space Mission Bible Camp a highflying success. Use the following suggestions to involve teenagers (or college students) in your program:

● **Have them act as Flight Crew Leaders.** Many young adults have younger siblings or baby-sit frequently and are comfortable working with children. Young adults will have a great time leading their crews—and will love how easy it is. (Teenagers will actually get as much out of the Bible stories and discussions as the young children will!)

● **Let teenagers and young adults help with registration.** Believe it or not, some young people have excellent organizational skills. These young people will enjoy forming crews, greeting children, and helping kids find their Flight Crew Leaders. After the first day, your registration helpers can register newcomers, count the daily attendance and report the number to the Mission Munchies Leader, and fill in for crew leaders who are absent.

● **Have qualified teenagers run your sound system or act as photographers.** Some high school drama programs train young people how to run sound, lighting, and video equipment. These teenagers make excellent Space Mission Bible Camp technical-staff members. You may even ask them to put together a slide show or video production of your program!

● **Ask teenagers to act as Bible Exploration volunteers.** The Bible Exploration Leader will need several volunteers to act as Bible characters in simple dramas. Teenagers with dramatic flair will enjoy playing Hannah, Peninnah, Thomas, Andrew, or prison guards.

● **If your youth group has a choir or worship band, let it help with Sing & Play Blast Off and Mission Send-Off Show Time.** Kids at Space Mission Bible Camp will love singing with the "big kids," and young adults will never have such a receptive and friendly audience again! Your Training Station Leaders will enjoy the extra backup and enthusiasm. Plus teenagers will learn and grow right along with the children!

There are countless ways to involve youth in Space Mission Bible Camp. Just let teenagers fill in where their gifts, talents, or interests lead them! You'll be surprised at how committed and enthusiastic these young volunteers are.

Pilot Program Pointer

We've discovered that younger children really look up to teenagers and young adults. In fact, you may find that crew members and teenage Flight Crew Leaders form close friendships and work well together. We frequently saw high school age crew leaders letting crew members wear their crew leader caps. Crew members thought they were hot stuff!

Spaceship Tip

You'll want to provide a Space Mission sticker sheet for each child (elementary and preschool) at your VBS. These sticker sheets include all the stickers kids will need for crafts and for their "Bible Blast Off" posters. Kids will love the bright, fun designs…and you'll love finding everything in one place!

What's a Student Book?

Each child at Space Mission Bible Camp will need a Student Book. The Student Book includes five Mission Logbooks to help kids accomplish their mission of God's love each day. Training Station Leaders at Have-a-Blast Games, Chadder's Space Mission Theater, Space Crafts, and Bible Exploration will use a special stamp to mark sections of each child's Mission Logbook. Each Mission Logbook includes a take-home newsletter filled with ways kids can continue their mission at home, remember the key Bible verse, and dive deeper into the Bible Point they've learned that day.

Each Student Book also contains a tear-out, foldout "Bible Blast Off" poster that kids will use to chart their progress in accomplishing their mission of God's love. The Chadder's Space Mission Theater Leader will hang the posters in the Sing & Play Blast Off area, and crew leaders will add stickers when kids report a "mission accomplished!" After Space Mission Bible Camp, kids can take the posters home and use them as growth charts. As they read the Scriptures at each growth mark, kids will be growing spiritually as well as physically! As an added bonus, we've included each Bible story on the back of the posters. The stories are written in an interactive, fun style for families to enjoy at home.

Preschoolers have their own age-appropriate Student Book, complete with five Mission Logbooks and a foldout "Bible Blast Off" poster just for them. The preschool Mission Logbooks include a daily Bible story activity page that children will use during Preschool Bible SpacePlace. Preschoolers' parents will appreciate the take-home newsletters—full of easy follow-up ideas, fun Bible-learning songs, and simple crafts that reinforce each day's Bible story and Point. Families will also enjoy the interactive Bible stories on the back of the "Bible Blast Off" poster!

Preschoolers will look forward to adding stickers and the Preschool Bible SpacePlace stamp to *their* "Bible Blast Off" posters. The Preschool Bible SpacePlace Director Manual suggests ways children can add something new to their posters each day. And, like the big kids, preschoolers can use their posters as growth charts (and Scripture-learning tools!) after VBS.

What Are Brite-Tites™?

Brite-Tites are nylon hosiery that have countless uses! At Space Mission Bible Camp, kids will enjoy using Brite-Tites in Have-a-Blast Games, Bible Exploration, and Preschool Bible SpacePlace. You'll be amazed at the versatility of this stretchy, durable material!

● Preschoolers will use Brite-Tites to act out the story of Hannah, decorate a variety of crafts, and create shiny Follow-Me Comets.

● Kids in Have-a-Blast Games will pass, toss, stretch, and tie Brite-Tites in a variety of games. They'll create a Brite-Tite "Superbat" for a game that will help them discover that with God's help, they can do seemingly impossible things.

● At Bible Exploration, Brite-Tites will become safe and simple handcuffs during the story of Paul and Silas in jail. This provides an easy and nonthreatening way for children to experience a little of the discomfort Paul and Silas felt.

Kids will be surprised at all the places Brite-Tites pop up at Space Mission Bible Camp!

Spaceship Tip

If you used Group's Vacation Bible Ship™, you'll recognize Brite-Tites! Many people enjoyed using this unique item for crafts, so we decided to show you even more ways to use Brite-Tites.

Who Is
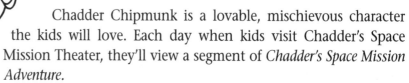
Chadder Chipmunk™?

Chadder Chipmunk is a lovable, mischievous character the kids will love. Each day when kids visit Chadder's Space Mission Theater, they'll view a segment of *Chadder's Space Mission Adventure.*

Kids will enjoy exploring Space Mission Bible Camp with Chadder as he relies on God's help to get along with an Exterminator who wants to get rid of Chadder! Though children of all ages will laugh at Chadder's antics as he's lured into the Exterminator's numerous traps, they'll also discover important Bible truths that apply to everyday life.

On Day 1, Chadder arrives at Space Mission Bible Camp excited to learn all about space travel. Unfortunately, the Exterminator targets him as a pesky rodent and sets out to do away with him. Nikki, a camp counselor, teaches Chadder that God helps us to be kind even when others are mean. She also shows Chadder that God helps us to be thankful in hard times, and that we can help others. With the help of former astronaut Jake Armstrong, Chadder rescues the Exterminator from danger, and Chadder and the Exterminator become friends.

The Chadder's Space Mission Theater Leader Manual contains discussion questions and activities that go along with each day's segment of *Chadder's Space Mission Adventure.* The video is available from Group Publishing and your local Christian bookstore.

Spaceship Tip

Your kids will love Chadder and will look forward to seeing him! Not only will they enjoy the twists and turns of the story, but they'll appreciate the wonderful downtime during a busy day at Space Mission Bible Camp. Kids are so active during VBS that it's nice for them to have a few moments to sit down, cool off, and relax. (Your Flight Crew Leaders will appreciate it, too!)

Can Kids Really Make Their Own Snacks?

Each day at Space Mission Bible Camp, a different group of kids will prepare snacks for the entire VBS. Snack preparation provides kids a unique opportunity to share God's mission of love by serving others. And it makes your job easier because you don't have to recruit additional volunteers to make snacks.

Believe it or not, one-fourth of your kids *can* prepare snacks for everyone else—if you follow the field-tested, step-by-step instructions provided in the Mission Munchies Leader Manual. Each day, snack preparation will follow the simple procedures outlined below.

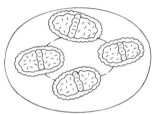

1. Before kids arrive, the Mission Munchies Leader sets out supplies according to the diagrams provided in the Mission Munchies Leader Manual.

2. After kids arrive and wash their hands, the leader explains each step of the snack preparation and invites kids to choose which steps they'd like to work on.

3. Kids work in assembly lines to prepare the snacks. Flight Crew Leaders are assigned the more difficult tasks such as handling sharp knives or pouring drinks.

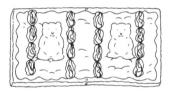

4. Kids set out the completed snacks on tables, where they'll be picked up and gobbled down during Mission Munchies.

Kids who serve on the Mission Munchies Service Crew report for snack preparation right after Sing & Play Blast Off. They'll take twenty to twenty-five minutes to prepare snacks before moving on to their next Training Station. And just in case kids don't finish in time, the Mission Munchies Leader has an additional twenty to twenty-five minutes to make final preparations before all the children arrive to eat. In Space Mission Bible Camp pilot programs, even preschoolers were able to complete their snack preparation within the allotted time!

As Mission Control Director, you'll want to drop in on the Mission Munchies Service Crew each day. Ask the leader how kids' work is progressing, and affirm the children for a job well done. But don't linger too long; you may distract kids from completing their work. Be sure to return at snack time to see children explain the meaning of the snack as *they* teach the Bible Point. Then watch the Mission Munchies Service Crew kids' faces light up as they're recognized for their accomplishment!

Pilot Program Pointer

In our pilot program, Mission Munchies Service became something kids really looked forward to. At the end of each day's Sing & Play Blast Off, the Mission Control Director would announce which group would be preparing the snack that day. You could hear the "lucky" kids whisper, "Yeah!" "All right!" or "That's us!" within their crews. We think it was terrific that kids looked forward to serving others.

Operation Kid-to-Kid™

A Hands-On
Mission of God's Love

What Is Operation Kid-to-Kid™?

God Had a Plan!

In developing Space Mission Bible Camp, the VBS team at Group Publishing wanted to include a meaningful service project that would help kids realize that with God's help, even children can impact the world! We wanted thousands of kids to join together and create something that would meet the needs of children across the world.

Well, God works in amazing ways! We met with a team from World Vision, a well-known Christian international relief agency. World Vision had tested a program in which churches sent school-supply kits to children in war-torn countries. These needy children had lost family members, friends, homes, churches, and schools. The school-supply kits not only had given children the tools to continue their education, but had also provided writing and drawing supplies to help children express and deal with the tremendous grief they were experiencing. The test program met with success, but World Vision wanted a vehicle that would take this mission project into churches everywhere. The partnership with Group's Space Mission Bible Camp and World Vision was a perfect fit, so we launched our VBS mission project, called Operation Kid-to-Kid!

How Your Kids Can Help

Each Flight Crew will put together a school pack containing the items pictured on page 36. On Day 2 of Space Crafts, Flight Crew members will work together to decide who will bring which items. Children will circle the items on their Operation Kid-to-Kid newsletters in their Student Books. (You'll find a similar handout on page 40 of this manual.) Since there are eight items, some children will need to bring more than one. We suggest "pairing up" less expensive items such as the eraser and the ruler or the pencil sharpener and the crayons. If parents can't provide an item, they'll circle the last paragraph on the handout and return it to you. For this reason, you'll need to have a few extra items on hand to fill in some packs. (Check out the ideas on page 37 to decide how your church and community members can provide the extras.)

On Day 5, the kids will use the resealable bags and photocopies of the "Gift of Love" handout from the Operation Kid-to-Kid packet (in the Starter Kit). Children will create their Operation Kid-to-Kid school packs in Space Crafts and then will keep the packs with them until Mission Send-Off Show Time. During

Pilot Program Pointer

We discovered that kids need a small-group setting to discuss, understand, and focus on Operation Kid-to-Kid. Space Crafts is a natural Operation Kid-to-Kid "headquarters." There, children learn about the project and its impact, choose their items, and create the school packs. In Space Crafts, kids also "meet" three children (through "Operation Kid-to-Kid" posters) who are representative of the children who will receive the school packs.

the closing program, Flight Crews will bring their school packs forward as an offering to God. This is a powerful, moving ceremony. Kids and leaders will be amazed as they watch the "mountain" of gifts grow higher and higher. It's a very concrete way for kids to see that when we all give "a little bit of love," God uses it to go a long, long way!

After Space Mission Bible Camp, simply place the packs in a large, sturdy box and tape it shut. Affix the mailing label from the Operation Kid-to-Kid packet, and ship the box to the Kid-to-Kid Send-Off Center. They'll take care of the rest!

IMPORTANT Specifics

Since this program has been tested by World Vision, there are specific guidelines which *must* be followed to ensure that your school packs are delivered to the children who need them.

● **All items must be new and in their original packaging.** The children receiving these items seldom get anything new. Leaving items in their original packaging so children can unwrap them will create more excitement for the recipients.

● **Each kit must include precisely the same items** so that foreign customs officials examining the crates containing thousands of kits will not delay or prevent delivery. For example, all the pencils must be painted yellow, not different colors. The crayons must be in boxes of twenty-four, not in boxes of sixteen or forty-eight. Providing identical items also prevents some children from being disappointed because they didn't receive as much as other children.

● **Each set of school supplies must be placed in a one-gallon resealable plastic bag.** These bags allow foreign customs officials to see clearly what each pack contains. In your starter kit, we've provided thirty official Operation Kid-to-Kid bags. (You can order more from Group Publishing and your local Christian bookstore.)

● **Christian tracts or other Bible-teaching material should not be included.** Since Christianity is illegal in many countries, any Bible-related items could cause customs officials to confiscate the entire pack (or box of packs). The "Gift of Love" handouts explain that the school-supply packs are gifts of love from other children. (You may want to use this point to start a discussion about what it would be like to live where people couldn't worship or even talk about Jesus.)

Spaceship Tip

Some children may ask to add candy, stickers, or toys to the school packs. Commend kids for their generosity, but explain that children who didn't get such treasures in their packs would feel bad.

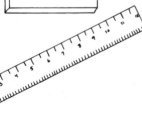

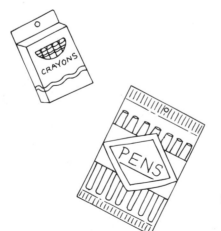

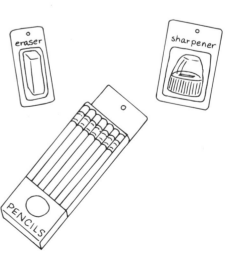

Operation Kid-to-Kid™ Countdown

Two Months Before Space Mission Bible Camp

● **Inform your congregation.** Photocopy the "We're Launching Kids on a Mission of God's Love!" bulletin insert (p. 41), and distribute it at a worship service. This handout explains Operation Kid-to-Kid and lets church members know how they can help.

● **Involve your congregation.** Church members can help by providing the extra items you'll need if kids aren't able or forget to bring their items. This is a super way to involve church members who can't give their time to Space Mission Bible Camp.

✔ Set a box in the church office to collect extra items to help fill the school-supply packs. Encourage church members to check the list in the bulletin and donate whatever items they can.

✔ Check with your college group, singles group, or senior citizens group to see if they'd be interested in trying to fill a small box with extra school-supply items. (Remember, the items must fit the descriptions on page 41.)

✔ Take a special offering to collect money to buy the necessary items. You can also use this money for shipping costs.

● **Involve your community.** Check with local discount stores or grocery stores to see if they would be willing to donate school-supply items for Operation Kid-to-Kid. They may actually donate enough items that children don't need to bring anything! You could also ask the stores to provide supplies for children whose families are unable to purchase items.

● **Consider setting up an Operation Kid-to-Kid "store"** if you live in a rural area where kids might have trouble getting these items on short notice. Gather enough items (from church members and donations from local merchants) for each Flight Crew to make an Operation Kid-to-Kid school pack. During Space Mission Bible Camp, display the items in a corner of your church. Allow children to purchase the item(s) they've chosen using real money or "mission money" you've distributed when kids carry out their daily missions.

Two Weeks Before Space Mission Bible Camp

● **Distribute supplemental supplies.** Give the Operation Kid-to-Kid bags and photocopies of the "Gift of Love" handout (from the Starter Kit) to the Preschool Bible SpacePlace Director and Space Crafts Leader. The Space Crafts

Spaceship Tip

"But what about the needy children at our church? I'm afraid many of them won't be able to afford any of the items." It's important for *all* children to understand that they can make a difference—regardless of social status or financial situation. Even if a child is unable to purchase his or her school supplies, provide extra items so children can place *something* in the kit. Children become empowered when they see themselves as part of the solution.

Spaceship Tip

You may want to provide another set of "Operation Kid-to-Kid" posters for your Preschool Bible SpacePlace. Preschoolers will enjoy "meeting" the children on the posters, too.

Operation Kid-to-Kid™

Leader will also need the three "Operation Kid-to-Kid" posters, available from Group Publishing and your local Christian bookstore.

● **Publicize your mission.** Photocopy the Operation Kid-to-Kid "News Release" on page 42, and fill in the information regarding your church's program. Send the news release to local newspapers, television, and radio stations so they can let others in your community know about your participation in Operation Kid-to-Kid.

During Space Mission Bible Camp

● **Remind kids to bring their items.** When the Sing & Play Blast Off Leader or Mission Send-Off Show Time Leader calls you up to make announcements, encourage kids to bring their items before Day 5.

● **Affirm kids when they accomplish their mission.** Each day, lead kids in cheering for those who've brought their school supplies. This positive reinforcement will be more powerful than all the nagging in the world!

● **Check in with Flight Crew Leaders.** During your opening huddle and prayer with the Flight Crew Leaders, ask them how their Operation Kid-to-Kid items are coming in. This will give you a feel for the number of extra items you might need at the end of the week.

After Space Mission Bible Camp

● **Send your school-supply packs to the Kid-to-Kid Send-Off Center.** Place your Operation Kid-to-Kid school packs in a large, sturdy packing box. Stuff the box with newspaper or newsprint to keep the items from shifting or possibly breaking. Tape the box shut, and affix the mailing label from the Operation Kid-to-Kid packet in your Starter Kit. (We've provided an offering envelope if your church wishes to take a donation to cover World Vision's shipping expenses or as a gift to the organization.)

● **Look for your Operation Kid-to-Kid update newsletter.** Several months after your program, World Vision will send your church a newsletter about Operation Kid-to-Kid. You'll learn how this outreach program affected thousands of children around the world. Share this powerful information with your children; they'll love hearing that their little bit of love went a long, long way!

● **Remind kids to visit the Operation Kid-to-Kid Web site.** Technology today will allow kids to chat with other Operation Kid-to-Kid participants and learn more about the countries where the school kits may be sent. Children can find more information about the Operation Kid-to-Kid Web site (www.ok2k.org) in their Student Books.

Operation Kid-to-Kid™

This newsletter, which is from kids' Student Books, contains information about Operation Kid-to-Kid and illustrates all the school supplies. It also includes a paragraph parents can circle if they can't buy supplies for Operation Kid-to-Kid. Kids will take their newsletters home on Day 2.

We're Launching Kids on a Mission of God's Love!

OPERATION Kid-to-Kid™

At Space Mission Bible Camp, your kids will take part in a hands-on mission project called Operation Kid-to-Kid™. With this project, kids will send school-supply packs to needy children around the world. The school-supply packs not only provide children in war-torn countries the items they need for continuing their education, but they also give children writing and drawing supplies that help them deal with the tremendous grief they've experienced.

Each Flight Crew (a group of five children who participate together in Space Mission Bible Camp activities) will create one school-supply pack containing eight new items still in their original packaging. **For customs regulations, each pack must contain exactly the same items.** Kids will work with their Flight Crews to decide who will bring which items. The school supply items are...

- a package of seven or eight yellow pencils;
- a package of ten ballpoint pens;
- two six-by-nine-inch steno pads with lined, white paper;
- a pencil sharpener;
- a pink gum eraser;
- a package of twenty-four crayons; and
- a twelve-inch ruler with metric markings.

If your child will be attending Space Mission Bible Camp, please wait to find out what he or she has chosen to bring before purchasing any items! Your child will bring home an information sheet, with the specific item(s) circled. If, however, you would like to donate extra items, please feel free to do so. We'll need extra school supplies for children who are unable to bring their own.

Contact _____ for more information.
                          VBS Director

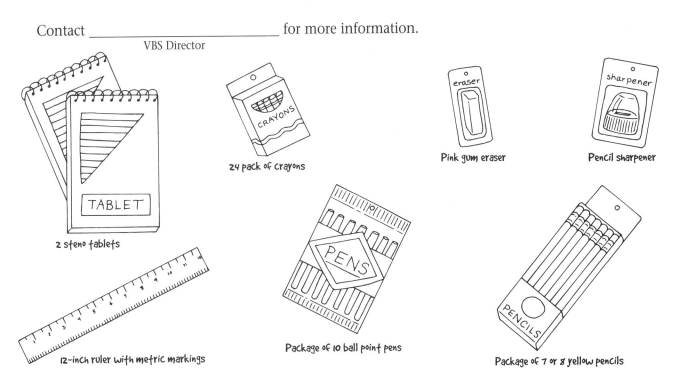

2 steno tablets

24 pack of crayons

Pink gum eraser

Pencil sharpener

12-inch ruler with metric markings

Package of 10 ball point pens

Package of 7 or 8 yellow pencils

Operation Kid-to-Kid™

News Release

Adapt the information in this news release to fit your church's Space Mission Bible Camp program. Then submit typed, double-spaced copies to your local newspapers, radio stations, and TV stations. You may want to check with them for any other specific requirements regarding news releases.

(Name of church) will be involved in a worldwide mission project called Operation Kid-to-Kid™. For this project, children attending (name of church)'s Space Mission Bible Camp will create school-supply packs to send to needy children around the world.

Operation Kid-to-Kid will show kids that with God's help, they can impact their world. Each child will be responsible for bringing one or two specific school-supply items such as steno pads, crayons, a pencil sharpener, or a ruler. Then small groups of children, called Flight Crews, will gather their items to create identical school-supply packs. The packs will be shipped to World Vision, an international relief organization, who will distribute them to children in war-torn countries such as Bosnia and Somalia.

Operation Kid-to-Kid is just one part of Space Mission Bible Camp, a program in which kids learn that God helps them in all aspects of life. Space Mission Bible Camp launches (starting date) and continues through (ending date). It's located at (name of church and church address). Space Station Sign-In opens each day at (starting time) and closes at (ending time). For more information, call (church phone number).

Planning Your Space Mission Bible Camp

How to create an "Out-of-This-World" Space Place

Planning
Countdown Calendar

 ## Three to Six Months Before
Space Mission Bible Camp

○ **Begin praying for your church's Space Mission Bible Camp.** Ask God to prepare the hearts of church members, workers, and children who will attend.

○ **Choose a format for your Space Mission Bible Camp.**
- ✔ Will you meet in the morning or in the evening?
- ✔ Will you meet every day for a week or once a week for several weeks?
- ✔ Will your program be for children only or will entire families be invited to attend?
- ✔ Will you meet at your church or another location?

○ **Set Space Mission Bible Camp dates.** As you're considering dates, you may want to find out about other summer programs offered by your church or your community so you can avoid conflicts.

○ **Choose a Mission Control Director.** If you're reading this manual, that's you! The director will be responsible for planning, recruiting staff, and overseeing all details to ensure that Space Mission Bible Camp goes smoothly.

○ **Set a budget.** Your church may already include VBS in its budget. If so, find out what funds are available. If your church doesn't have a VBS budget in place, consider the following ideas:
- ✔ Collect an offering to cover expenses.
- ✔ Charge a per-child registration fee for Space Mission Bible Camp. Give discounts to families that register more than one child.
- ✔ Invite congregation members to "sponsor" children by contributing a per-child amount.

Two to Three Months Before Space Mission Bible Camp

❍ **Plan Space Mission Bible Camp publicity.** Decide how you'll promote Space Mission Bible Camp in your church and community. Refer to the "Publicity: Getting Your Church and Community on the Launch Pad" section (pp. 117-129) in this manual for publicity ideas and resources.

❍ **Begin recruiting Training Station Leaders.** Photocopy the leader job descriptions (pp. 83-90). Give the job descriptions to people in your church who'd enjoy leading that Training Station. Or post the job descriptions on a large bulletin board you've covered with foil, stars, or pictures of spacecraft. As you talk to people, focus on the job descriptions rather than on previous church teaching experience. A restaurant chef who's never taught Sunday school might make a great Mission Munchies Leader!

You might want to announce your staffing needs in a worship service. Then post the job descriptions on a large sheet of poster board under the heading "Mission: To Help Launch Kids on a Mission of God's Love." People can sign their names on the job descriptions they're interested in. It's OK if more than one person signs up for each Training Station.

❍ **Estimate your Space Mission Bible Camp enrollment.** Use figures from your church's Sunday school or figures from last year's VBS program. Once you've estimated how many children will attend, figure out how many Flight Crew Leaders you'll need. You'll need one adult or teenage Flight Crew Leader for every five children, including preschoolers. Be sure to have extra Flight Crew Leaders ready in case you need to form Flight Crews from last-minute registrants.

❍ **Order Space Mission Bible Camp materials.** If you purchased the Space Mission Bible Camp Starter Kit, you already have a leader manual for every Training Station. You may want to order additional leader manuals for team teaching. Your Chadder's Space Mission Theater Leader will need a copy of the *Chadder's Space Mission Adventure* video.

For every elementary-age child, you'll *need* to order...
- ✔ an Elementary Student Book;
- ✔ an elementary Space Mission sticker sheet; and
- ✔ craft items:
  - ✔ a Tube-a-loon Rocket Kit,
  - ✔ three yards of space lace,
  - ✔ a Blast Off Rocket Kit, and
  - ✔ a Talkie Tapes strip.

For every preschooler, you'll *need* to order...
- ✔ a Preschool Student Book;
- ✔ a preschool Space Mission sticker sheet; and
- ✔ craft items:
  - ✔ three yards of space lace and
  - ✔ a Tube-a-loon Rocket Kit.

Even if you're planning a late-summer program, it's not too early to order materials! As you update your registration count, you can order additional student supplies as needed.

Spaceship Tip

One yard of glow-in-the-dark space lace will be used to string children's name badges. The other two yards will be used for crafts.

○ **Survey your church facilities.** Make preliminary Training Station area assignments. You'll need to set up a separate room or area for each station. Use the following guidelines.

Spaceship Tip

If your plans involve more than 150 children, consider running two or more simultaneous Training Stations. For more information on how to do this, see "What's a Training Station?" on page 22.

○ **Sing & Play Blast Off**
- ✔ large room to accommodate entire Space Mission Bible Camp (possibly a sanctuary or fellowship hall)
- ✔ sound system/microphone (helpful)
- ✔ outlet to plug in audiocassette player or CD player (or a sound system to play *Sing & Play Blast Off* audiocassette or CD)
- ✔ outlet to plug in overhead projector (if using *Sing & Play Blast Off Lyrics Transparencies)*
- ✔ outlet to plug in TV/VCR (if using *Sing & Play Blast Off Music Video)*

○ **Chadder's Space Mission Theater**
- ✔ classroom to accommodate all the preschoolers at once and to accommodate one-fourth of elementary-age kids (helpful if room can be darkened)
- ✔ outlet to plug in TV/VCR

○ **Space Crafts**
- ✔ classroom to accommodate one-fourth of elementary-age kids (carpeted floor is OK—no glue, glitter, or other messy supplies will be used)
- ✔ one or two low tables (helpful)
- ✔ outlet to plug in audiocassette player or CD player if using *Sing & Play Blast Off* audiocassette or CD

○ **Mission Munchies**
- ✔ large room to accommodate entire Space Mission Bible Camp (possibly a fellowship hall or gymnasium)
- ✔ church kitchen or other noncarpeted area for Mission Munchies Service

○ **Have-a-Blast Games**
- ✔ room or outdoor area to accommodate one-fourth of elementary-age kids (a fellowship hall, gymnasium, lawn, or parking lot)
- ✔ room for children to run around
- ✔ outlet to plug in audiocassette player or CD player if using *Sing & Play Blast Off* audiocassette or CD

Pilot Program Pointer

We had children pick up their snacks inside after praying together and learning the meaning of the snack. Then children went directly outside to eat. This was less messy, gave children the opportunity to enjoy the sunshine, and provided a few crumbs for the birds!

○ **Bible Exploration**
- ✔ classroom that can accommodate one-fourth of elementary-age kids and that can be darkened
- ✔ classroom that's larger than ten feet by twenty-five feet
- ✔ classroom that's in a quiet area of your facility (helpful for storytelling, especially on Day 4)
- ✔ outlet to plug in audiocassette player

Planning Your Space Mission Bible Camp

○ **Mission Send-Off Show Time**
  ✔ large room to accommodate entire Space Mission Bible Camp (possibly a sanctuary or fellowship hall; could use the same room as Sing & Play Blast Off)
  ✔ sound system/microphone (helpful)
  ✔ outlet to plug in audiocassette player
  ✔ stage (helpful)

○ **Preschool Bible SpacePlace**
  ✔ classroom(s) to accommodate all preschoolers
  ✔ outlet to plug in audiocassette player
  ✔ restroom facilities in room or nearby
  ✔ child-sized furniture
  ✔ preschool toys such as blocks, modeling dough, dress-up clothes, and stuffed animals

Spaceship Tip

Since preschoolers work at learning centers or stations, you may want to set up one room for these stations and use another place for storytelling and singing.

○ **Plan and schedule a leader training meeting using the " 'Blast Off!' Leader Training Meeting" (pp. 102-110).** This outline incorporates the *Countdown!* video, which contains clips from Space Mission Bible Camp pilot programs. Your Training Station Leaders will enjoy seeing Space Mission Bible Camp in action. Be sure to include Flight Crew Leaders in your training so they can better understand their role. The *Countdown!* video includes information just for crew leaders that explains their duties and describes how to be effective in discussions and with discipline.

Plan to meet for at least two hours.

Eight Weeks Before Space Mission Bible Camp

○ **Begin recruiting Flight Crew Leaders.** Flight Crew Leaders are like older brothers and sisters in the Flight Crew family. They aren't responsible for teaching, and they don't have to prepare anything. Flight Crew Leaders can be teenagers, college students, parents, or grandparents. They need only to love the Lord and love children.

For elementary-age crews, Flight Crew Leaders should have completed junior high school. For preschool crews, Flight Crew Leaders should have completed elementary school. This is a great way to involve kids who feel they're "too old" for VBS themselves. Flight Crew Leaders should plan to participate in Space Mission Bible Camp for the entire program. If they need to be absent one or more days, encourage them to find their own substitutes.

○ **Begin publicity.** Fill in your program's dates and times on the Space Mission Bible Camp outdoor banner (available from Group Publishing and your local Christian bookstore). Display the banner in a prominent outdoor location.

Hang Space Mission Bible Camp theme posters (available from Group

Publishing and your local Christian bookstore) in your church and community.

Show the promotional segment of the *Countdown!* video during a worship service or other church gathering. This five-minute segment, found at the beginning of your *Countdown!* video, shows scenes from actual Space Mission Bible Camp programs. You'll find that the video helps build enthusiasm, recruit volunteers, and promote attendance for your program.

○ **Prepare your church members for Operation Kid-to-Kid.** Photocopy the "We're Launching Kids on a Mission of God's Love!" bulletin insert (p. 41), and distribute it to all adults. This flier gives information about Operation Kid-to-Kid and explains how members of your congregation can donate items. It also gives parents a "heads-up" so they know what's coming.

○ **Begin gathering supplies.** Refer to the master supply list, "Supplies: Everything You Need for a Successful Mission" (p. 61). Consult with Training Station Leaders to inform them of how you'll handle supply collection. Will you gather all supplies or will each leader gather his or her own supplies? You may want to ask church members to donate food supplies (such as peanut butter, graham crackers, or gummy bears) or easy-to-find items (such as paper grocery sacks, newspaper, or robes).

○ **Plan your Space Mission Bible Camp schedule.** The average VBS program runs for up to three hours each day. Group's Space Mission Bible Camp materials have been developed with these parameters in mind. For a three-hour program, Sing & Play Blast Off and Mission Munchies should last fifteen minutes apiece, and every other Training Station should last twenty-five minutes. See the daily schedules on pages 70-78 to see how this works. If your program will meet for more or less time than three hours each day, you'll need to adapt these times accordingly.

Four Weeks Before Space Mission Bible Camp

○ **Recruit additional volunteers.** In addition to Training Station Leaders and Flight Crew Leaders, you may want to recruit volunteers to help with registration, transportation, photography, and child care for the staff.

○ **Continue publicity.** Mail Space Mission Bible Camp invitation postcards to children in your church and community. Distribute Space Mission Bible Camp doorknob danglers in your community. Write your church's name and when your Space Mission Bible Camp will blast off.

○ **Begin preregistration.** Photocopy the "Space Mission Bible Camp Registration Form" (p. 148), or purchase Space Mission Bible Camp registration cards (available from Group Publishing and your local Christian bookstore). Insert copies in your church bulletins, distribute copies in Sunday school classes, and keep a supply in your church office. Encourage parents from your church to

Spaceship Tip

For an eye-catching registration display, remove the lid from your Space Mission Bible Camp Starter Kit can. Then use poster board to create a cone-shaped "nose" that will fit on top of your Starter Kit can to transform it into a registration "rocket." Cover the poster board with foil for an extra "space-y" effect. Make a slit in the poster board so kids and parents can slip their registration forms into the rocket. You can even provide shiny pencils that look metallic or holographic for parents to use to fill out their registration forms.

preregister their children and their children's friends. This will make your first day more manageable.

○ **Hold the scheduled leader training meeting.** Plan to meet in a large room where you'll be able to try out some Space Mission Bible Camp snacks and activities. If possible, meet in the room you'll use for Bible Exploration so Training Station Leaders and Flight Crew Leaders can help build the paper bag pit there. Before the meeting, set up a TV and VCR and decorate the room using the suggestions provided in the leader training outline (p. 102). Bring the Training Station leader manuals, Training Station stamps, and photocopies of the "For Flight Crew Leaders Only" handouts (pp. 111-116). Don't forget to provide yummy Mission Munchies for your workers!

○ **Provide Space Mission Bible Camp information to your church office.** Fill in your church's information on the community flier on page 127, and photocopy a stack of complete fliers on brightly colored paper to put in your church office. Someone in the office can refer to the fliers if people call with questions about your program and can distribute fliers to people who stop by the office.

If your church has a phone answering machine, you may also want to include Space Mission Bible Camp information in your recorded message. If your church has its own Web site, be sure to add Space Mission Bible Camp information there, too.

Two Weeks Before Space Mission Bible Camp

○ **Check your registration count.** Make sure you have enough Student Books and Space Mission sticker sheets for each child to have one. Order extras just in case; many churches experience last-minute add-ons, first-day surprises, and unexpected increases as kids bring their friends throughout the week. Also double-check that you have enough Flight Crew Leaders, assigning one crew leader to five children.

○ **Check your supply collection.** Make a final announcement or put a final supply list in your church bulletin. Gather or purchase additional supplies as necessary.

○ **Continue publicity.** Photocopy and fill out the news release (p. 126), and send copies to your local newspapers, radio stations, and TV stations. Use the snazzy clip art found on the *Sing & Play Blast Off Music & Clip Art CD* to create fliers, bulletins, posters, and more! This CD contains the thirteen upbeat Sing & Play Blast Off songs and works with Macintosh and PC-compatible computers.

Announce Space Mission Bible Camp in worship services and other church gatherings. Put bulletin inserts and table tents (pp. 123-124) in your church's worship bulletins.

As church members enter your facility, distribute theme-oriented snacks such as snack-sized Milky Way or Mars candy bars, Starburst fruit chews, or Astro Pops. Attach a message such as "Come and be a star at Space Mission Bible Camp!"

Spaceship Tip

It's a good idea to line up a few extra Flight Crew Leaders who will be available in case you have lots of walk-in registrants. Be sure these Flight Crew Leaders arrive early on Day 1 so they can step in if necessary. (Because no preparation is needed for Flight Crew Leaders, it's easy for people to step in at any point.)

Before your worship service, have a few volunteers perform the publicity skit on pages 128-129. Show the promotional segment of the *Countdown!* video again.

Mail additional Space Mission Bible Camp invitation postcards as necessary.

○ **Make backup and emergency plans.** What if it rains during your program? Plan in advance how you'll handle bad weather. You may also want to line up backup Flight Crew Leaders in case some drop out.

Inform Training Station Leaders and Flight Crew Leaders of procedures you'll follow if there's a fire or other emergency.

One Week Before Space Mission Bible Camp

○ **Dedicate Space Mission Bible Camp staff.** Introduce Training Station Leaders, Flight Crew Leaders, and other volunteers during your church service. Then have your pastor or other church members pray that God will use these workers to touch kids' lives with his love during Space Mission Bible Camp.

○ **Assign kids to Flight Crews.** Photocopy the "Flight Crew Roster" (p. 146). You'll need one roster for each Flight Crew. Using the preregistration forms you've received, assign children to elementary and preschool Flight Crews. Each Flight Crew should have no more than five children and one adult or teenage Flight Crew Leader. Be sure that each preschool Flight Crew has a mix of three-, four-, and five-year-olds.

Here are some additional guidelines for assigning crews:

✔ Fill in the "Flight Crew Roster" (p. 146) in pencil—you'll probably make changes as you work.

✔ Whenever possible, place a child from each age level in each Flight Crew. If the age distribution at your program is uneven, include as wide an age range as you can. Avoid forming single-age Flight Crews.

✔ If a child is bringing a friend, assign the two children to the same Flight Crew if possible. If a child is bringing several friends, assign pairs of kids to different Flight Crews.

✔ In general, it works best to assign siblings to different Flight Crews. However, you know the children in your church. Use your judgment as to whether siblings should be together.

✔ If you anticipate behavior problems with certain children, assign them to Flight Crews that will have more experienced adult Flight Crew Leaders.

✔ If you have children who are particularly helpful or cooperative, assign them to Flight Crews that will have teenage Flight Crew Leaders.

✔ If you want your program to have a strong outreach emphasis, limit each Flight Crew to three or four children. Then encourage kids to fill their crews by bringing their friends!

✔ Remember to leave open spaces in a few crews for kids who haven't preregistered.

Pilot Program Pointer

Our Training Station Leaders needed a way to quickly identify the Flight Crew Leaders in each group. We provided Space Mission Bible Camp caps for the crew leaders to wear during the week. Many crew leaders wrote their names on their caps, used markers to decorate their caps, or had their Flight Crew members sign their caps. The caps turned into fun souvenirs for crew leaders to take home at the end of the week. Space Mission Bible Camp caps are available from Group Publishing and your local Christian bookstore.

Pilot Program Pointer

We've received countless letters from Group VBS customers who've admitted they were skeptical about forming combined-age crews. But when these customers took a leap of faith and tried combined-age crews, they were amazed at how well they worked! Most people noted a decline in discipline problems, an increase in cooperation, and a special bonding among crew members.

✔ After you've assigned elementary children to Flight Crews, assign each crew to one of four larger groups. (Remember, one-fourth of the kids at VBS travel together at a time.) Label these four groups A, B, C, and D— or use your creativity to name them something that fits the space theme, such as Radical Rockets or Cool Comets. Flight Crews will travel with their larger groups as they visit the Training Stations each day. For more information about assigning Flight Crews to groups, see page 135.

✔ Once you've finished assigning crews, double-check that you haven't forgotten anyone or double-booked anyone.

○ **Meet with Training Station Leaders.** Check with each station leader to make sure he or she has all the required supplies, and answer any questions he or she may have. Work together to smooth out any last-minute details.

○ **Decide when and where Training Station Leaders and Flight Crew Leaders will meet at Space Mission Bible Camp each day.** You may want to have your staff arrive early on Day 1 to greet children and assist with registration. Be sure each Flight Crew Leader has a large sign with his or her crew number written on it.

○ **Help Training Station Leaders decorate their rooms.** Use the decorating ideas found in the leader manuals or the general decorating suggestions in the "Facilities: Turn Your Church Into a Space Training Center" section of this manual (pp. 58-61) to create an "out-of-this-world" atmosphere.

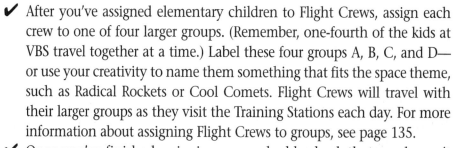

During Space Mission Bible Camp

○ **Meet with Flight Crew Leaders during Sing & Play Blast Off.** Each day the Sing & Play Blast Off Leader will excuse Flight Crew Leaders for a quick huddle and prayer with you outside the Sing & Play Blast Off area. This is a great time to ask crew leaders if they have any needs or concerns, make last-minute announcements or schedule changes, and encourage your crew leaders. Lead a prayer, asking God to bless your day, protect everyone, and give all leaders wisdom as they work with each child.

○ **Register new children.** Make sure you have plenty of workers on hand to register kids the first day! (This is an excellent way to use volunteers who aren't available to help the entire week.) Set up separate registration stations for preregistration check-in and walk-in registration. Follow the Day 1 registration procedures outlined on pages 139-144.

After Day 1, maintain a registration table to register kids who join your program "midflight."

○ **Meet with Training Station Leaders and Flight Crew Leaders after each day's program.** Check in with all Space Mission Bible Camp staff

Pilot Program Pointer

In our pilot program, it worked well to have Flight Crew Leaders arrive at least ten to fifteen minutes early each day. Each crew leader picked up a daily schedule and then waited in his or her crew area in Sing & Play Blast Off. This made it easy for kids to find their crew leaders and settle in right away.

Pilot Program Pointer

The huddle and prayer time proved to be helpful for everyone. For example, when a teenage crew leader shared that she was having trouble with one of her crew members, an older crew leader mentioned that she had a small crew and would be glad to have the two groups combine. Since we caught the situation early, the "combo crew" (and its leaders) had a fantastic week! Also, seeing their leaders pray for them was a great model for children.

to see what went smoothly and what could be improved for future days. Be prepared to change schedules, rooms, or procedures! You may even need to reassign some Flight Crews. Work together to make any necessary changes to ensure that everything runs smoothly.

○ **Give announcements during Sing & Play Blast Off or Mission Send-Off Show Time.** During the course of the program, you may need to change schedules, locations, or Flight Crew assignments. You also may have personal messages or lost-and-found items to deliver to participants. Each day, check with the Sing & Play Blast Off Leader and Mission Send-Off Show Time Leader to schedule any announcements you'd like everyone to hear.

○ **Attend Sing & Play Blast Off and Mission Send-Off Show Time each day.** These opening and closing activities will give you a good indication of how your mission is proceeding. They also provide opportunities for children to see you and to identify you as the Mission Control Director. On Day 1, you'll announce Flight Crew group assignments (A, B, C, D) and will join other staff members in teaching children the motions to "Little Bit of Love." Each day, the Sing & Play Blast Off Leader may call on you to pray before dismissing kids to their Training Stations. Besides, you'll have fun!

○ **Make sure all Training Station Leaders and Flight Crew Leaders are present each day.** Arrange for substitutes if necessary. If you're in a pinch for Flight Crew Leaders, ask the Sing & Play Blast Off Leader and Mission Send-Off Show Time Leader to fill in—or appoint yourself crew leader for a day.

○ **Make sure Training Station Leaders and Flight Crew Leaders have the supplies they need each day.** Have a runner available to collect or purchase additional supplies if necessary.

○ **Help with discipline problems as necessary.** In Space Mission Bible Camp pilot programs, workers encountered virtually no discipline problems. Each day was so full of fun Bible-learning activities that kids didn't have time to misbehave. Combined-age Flight Crews encourage kids to work together instead of squabble, and minor problems can be handled by Training Station Leaders or Flight Crew Leaders.

○ **Stock and maintain a first-aid station.** Keep a good supply of adhesive bandages and first-aid ointment on hand along with phone numbers for local clinics and hospitals. You may also want to keep photocopies of kids' registration forms near your first-aid station. You can use the forms to check for allergies or other health concerns.

○ **Prepare Space Mission Bible Camp completion certificates for your "astronauts."** Photocopy and fill out a "Mission Accomplished!" certificate (p. 169) for each child. Space Mission Bible Camp completion certificates are also available from Group Publishing and your local Christian bookstore.

Pilot Program Pointer

During our pilot program, we met each afternoon for prayer and lunch and to talk about the highlights of the day. This was a fun time for volunteers to relax and share stories about what had happened during their Training Stations or about what the kids in their Flight Crews had done. Not only did we glean important information (to include in the finished program), but it gave everyone a peek at the other exciting things going on at Space Mission Bible Camp.

Spaceship Tip

It's important to check your registration forms for any mention of food allergies. Let the Mission Munchies Leader know as soon as possible so he or she can make alternative snacks if necessary.

# After Space Mission Bible Camp

○ **Collect reusable leftover supplies.** Store the supplies in your church's supply closet or resource room for use in future VBS programs or other children's ministry events. If you borrowed supplies such as buckets, laundry baskets, or cassette players, return them to their owners.

○ **Send your Operation Kid-to-Kid school packs to the Kid-to-Kid Send-Off Center.** Place the completed school-supply packs in a large, sturdy box. Be sure to stuff crumpled newspaper or newsprint in any open areas so the box is packed tightly. Tape the box shut, and then simply affix the mailing label from the Operation Kid-to-Kid packet. World Vision will distribute your school-supply packs around the world! (For more information, see the "Operation Kid-to-Kid" section on pages 33-42.)

○ **Leave rooms decorated for your next church service.** If outreach was an emphasis during Space Mission Bible Camp, you'll be pleased when visitors from your VBS program come for church. They'll feel more comfortable returning to a familiar environment. Also, church members will enjoy getting a glimpse of Space Mission Bible Camp.

○ **Follow up with Space Mission Bible Camp visitors.** Mail Space Mission Bible Camp follow-up postcards (available from Group Publishing and your local Christian bookstore). Encourage Flight Crew Leaders to make personal contact with the members of their Flight Crews within two weeks after Space Mission Bible Camp. Use the additional follow-up ideas on pages 166-167 in this manual.

○ **Report on your program.** During your next worship service, invite Training Station Leaders, Flight Crew Leaders, and kids who attended Space Mission Bible Camp to share their favorite VBS experiences. Encourage kids to display their Space Crafts. You may even want to invite the Sing & Play Blast Off Leader to lead everyone in singing one or two favorite Space Mission Bible Camp songs.

○ **Present a slide show or post photos from your program.** Kids (and their parents) love seeing themselves on the "big screen." And colorful photos will bring back memories of a terrific time at Space Mission Bible Camp.

○ **Meet with your entire Space Mission Bible Camp staff to evaluate your program.** Make written notes of good ideas that could be used for next year's program. Note any problems that came up and how they were solved. Brainstorm about ways to avoid similar problems in the future. Include notes of how you adapted the Space Mission Bible Camp materials to fit your church. Record the names of Flight Crew Leaders and Training Station Leaders who might be interested in helping again next year. Bring the Space Mission Bible Camp evaluation forms included in this manual (pp. 172-173), and have staff members fill them out.

○ **Thank your staff for all their hard work.** Photocopy and fill out a "Mission Accomplished!" certificate (p. 168) for each Training Station Leader, Flight Crew Leader, and other volunteers. Or use the Space Mission Bible Camp thank you cards and certificates available from Group Publishing and your local Christian bookstore. You could even hand out balloons, flowers, or baked goodies to show your appreciation.

○ **Fill out the "Space Mission Bible Camp Evaluation."** Tear out this evaluation form (pp. 175-176), and fill it out completely. Send your completed form to Group Publishing—no postage is necessary! You may also want to give a copy of the form to your church pastor, Christian education director, children's minister, or VBS committee. This helps us plan for the future!

When and Where to Launch Your Space Mission

If your church has put on VBS programs before, you probably have a good idea of the times and settings that work best in your situation. Group's Space Mission Bible Camp works in just about any setting—midweek clubs, day camps, and traditional five-day settings. Use the suggested times and settings listed below to spark creativity as you plan your Space Mission Bible Camp program.

Options for Space Mission Bible Camp Locations

● **Your church:** Many VBS programs are held in local churches. With this approach, you control the facilities, how many rooms are available, and the location is familiar to church members. Plus, visitors who come to Space Mission Bible Camp will actually visit your church site.

● **A local park:** Kids love being outdoors, and parks draw children who would not normally attend a VBS program. Check with your local parks and recreation department to see about reserving a park or campground for your Space Mission Bible Camp. Church, YMCA, and scout camps provide ideal outdoor settings since they usually have electricity available.

● **Inner city:** Turn your Space Mission Bible Camp program into an inner city outreach opportunity. Invite kids from your church to join inner city kids in an inner city church or neighborhood setting. Even if you use only portions of the Space Mission Bible Camp materials, you'll launch an important mission of

God's love to needy children and their families.

● **A local school:** Since most schools lie dormant for the majority of the summer, consider using their facilities for your program. If public schools are busy with summer classes, check out Christian school facilities in your area.

Options for Space Mission Bible Camp Times

● **Weekday mornings:** Many programs are held for five consecutive weekday mornings. Kids have plenty of energy, and the summer sun isn't quite as hot as in the afternoon. For a change of pace, you could even plan to hold a morning program during your students' spring break!

● **Weekday evenings:** Since many church members work during the day, some churches find it easier to staff an evening program. This could be a special program that you hold for five consecutive days, or it could take the place of an existing midweek program. If you hold your Space Mission Bible Camp program in the evening, you may want to include families. You can offer separate programming for parents and teenagers or include them in Space Mission Bible Camp as full-fledged participants and Flight Crew Leaders. Church members of all ages will enjoy visiting the Training Stations! Each family can form its own Flight Crew, or you can mix families and enlist parents as Flight Crew Leaders. If you invite families, you'll want to provide child care for children younger than three years old.

● **Midweek clubs:** If your church has a midweek club or another weekly children's program, you may want to use the Space Mission Bible Camp materials for five consecutive weeks. If you use Space Mission Bible Camp during a regularly scheduled midweek program, you'll probably have Training Station Leaders already in place. Just assign Flight Crews and recruit Flight Crew Leaders, and you'll be ready to blast off!

● **Day camp:** Extend Space Mission Bible Camp to a half-day day camp for kids in your community. We've provided extra crafts, plenty of games, and lots of upbeat songs to keep children actively learning Bible truths...and having a great time!

● **Sunday mornings:** Hold Space Mission Bible Camp during your normal Sunday school or children's church time. This is a great change of pace for summer for both kids and children's workers.

● **Weekend retreat:** Invite children or whole families to participate in a weekend retreat held at your church or a local camp. Schedule Day 1 activities for Saturday morning, Days 2 and 3 for Saturday afternoon (after lunch), Day 4 for Saturday evening (after dinner), and Day 5 for Sunday morning. You'll need to let families know about Operation Kid-to-Kid ahead of time so they can bring their school supplies for the mission project.

for a Successful Space Mission...

The following tips will help your evening or intergenerational program go smoothly:

● Start early so young children won't get too tired.

● Consider beginning each session with a simple meal. Recruit a kitchen team to organize potlucks or prepare simple meals such as sandwiches or frozen pizzas. If your church has a lawn or grassy area nearby, you may even want to barbecue. Families will enjoy this casual interaction time, and you'll be able to start your program earlier.

● Make sure children who attend without their families have safe transportation to and from Space Mission Bible Camp. Don't allow children to walk home alone in the dark—even if they live nearby.

● Families come in all shapes and sizes. Be sensitive to single-parent families, childless couples, and children who come alone. You may want to assign family members to separate Flight Crews to avoid drawing attention to family differences.

Have fun as you chart the course that's best for your Space Mission Bible Camp!

Facilities: Turn Your Church Into a Space Training Center

Atmosphere and environment enhance learning, so decorations are an integral part of Space Mission Bible Camp. They can set the mood for the week and can get children excited about their mission of God's love. Following, you'll find a listing of suggested decorations for Training Stations and other church areas. Remember, these are options and aren't necessary for the success of your Space Mission Bible Camp. If you and others want to go the extra mile, it'll simply enhance the program.

Most decorating items can be found among your church members or can be purchased inexpensively. Have fun! Letting your imagination and creativity go wild, you can create a "sky's-the-limit" environment! Go for it!

Space Station Sign-In

This is your registration area. It will be kids' first impression of Space Mission Bible Camp. Create mystery and excitement by making it look like the entrance to a space shuttle or rocket.

● **Have costumed staff on hand.** Have volunteers dress up in flight suits, robot costumes, or astronaut "gear" to greet and welcome children each day. Use boxes (spray-painted silver), silver dryer ducts, "space blankets," and Christmas lights to pull together a simple robot costume.

● **Play an audiocassette of space noises.** Tape the sounds of household appliances such as a microwave oven, digital timer, computer, or push-button

Spaceship Tip

VBS Directors continue to amaze us with their creativity, hard work, and incredibly imaginative ideas! If you've jumped "light-years" ahead of us to transform your facility into an astronaut training center, we'd love to see how you did it! Please send pictures or videocassettes to the VBS Coordinator at Group Publishing, Inc., P.O. Box 481, Loveland, CO 80539. (Sorry, we can't return them!)

Planning Your Space Mission Bible Camp

58

telephone to create beeps, blips, whistles, and other high-tech sound effects. Or use a set of inexpensive walkie-talkies to record a static-filled conversation between an "astronaut" and "mission control." Make several copies of the audiocassette, and place an audiocassette player under each registration table.

● **Cover tables and doors with shiny space blankets.** Space blankets (large sheets of Mylar) are an easy way to turn plain doors, bookshelves, bulletin boards, and tables into shiny, sparkling, "space-y" objects! Space blankets are available from Group Publishing and your local Christian bookstore.

● **Create a dimly lit spaceport entry.** If possible, darken your entryway by covering walls and windows with black landscaping plastic. Use two rows of Christmas lights to make a path on the floor, guiding kids to Sing & Play Blast Off. Hang balloon "planets" or an inflatable globe around your entryway.

Pilot Program Pointer

We loved using space blankets in decorating! This lightweight, sturdy material provides a quick way to make any object look "space-y." Aluminum foil is also OK, but it's more expensive and tears easily.

Spacewalks

Even your hallways can be eye-catching and exciting! As children travel to their Training Stations, they'll feel as if they're really at an astronaut training center getting ready to blast off on an important mission.

● **Create a galaxy of stars.** To help kids feel as if they're walking in space, dim the lights in your hallways or replace your regular light bulbs with black-light bulbs (available from Group Publishing and your local Christian bookstore). Cover the walls with black paper or landscaping plastic. Then attach glow-in-the-dark star stickers to create constellations on your walls. To be sure kids can find their way in the dark, tape white Christmas lights to the floor, creating a path.

● **Photocopy and cut out the arrows from the back of the "Signs and Planning" poster.** You'll need at least two arrows per Training Station to guide children through your facility. Then cut the Training Station signs from the front of the poster, and hang the posters and arrows so kids can find their way to the correct Training Stations. (You may want to purchase extra posters so station leaders can post Training Station signs on their doors, too.)

Spaceship Tip

If you can't use black-light bulbs in your hallway lights, gather several desk lamps or floor lamps. Place the lamps against the hallway walls, and then replace the regular light bulbs with black-light bulbs. Kids will love the eerie glow of black light!

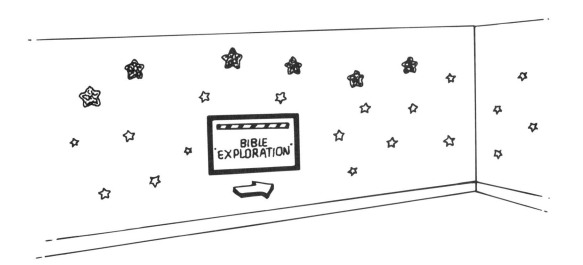

Spaceship Tip

Be sure to have your Flight Crew Leaders make poster board or construction paper number signs for each Flight Crew. Post each number on a different pew or row of chairs in Sing & Play Blast Off so Flight Crews know where to sit each day.

● **Hang shiny stars from the ceiling.** Shape stars from crumpled aluminum foil, and then use fishing wire or sewing thread to hang the stars at differing lengths from the ceiling. Although you want kids to enjoy the 3-D effect, make sure the stars are high enough that children can't hit or pull them.

Training Stations

Specific decorating ideas for each Training Station are listed in the individual leader manuals. Use the following ideas to reinforce the space theme in all of your Training Stations.

● **Create a "space scene" in each window.** Use black paper or landscaping plastic to cover windows, and then add glow-in-the-dark star stickers to create various constellations. Cut shapes of planets, rockets, satellites, and comets from Con-Tact paper, and add them to your "space scene." When kids look "out" the window, they'll feel as if they're really in outer space!

● **Hang posters of real spacecraft.** Most school-supply and science-specialty stores carry pictures of recent or historic space missions. Not only will these spectacular photos reinforce the space theme, but they will also please the kids.

● **Turn each door into a spaceport.** Use space blankets to "wrap" each Training Station door. Mylar gives doors an official look and becomes a quick visual to help kids recognize the area as a designated Training Station.

● **Let robot "friends" welcome children at every Training Station.** Use boxes sprayed with silver paint, silver dryer ducts, pie tins, garbage cans, and old appliances to create simple, stationary robots. Add warmth and friendliness to your Space Mission Bible Camp by having one robot stand at the door to each Training Station. Kids will love greeting the robots, and your simple creations will become beloved mascots! (You may want to ask middle schoolers and teenagers to creatively come up with robot ideas!)

● **String a solar system in the sky!** Use balloons, inflatable balls, or Styrofoam balls to make planets, moons...even a sun! Create Saturn's rings by cutting the center from a paper plate and then pushing the "planet" into the center of the ring. Use neon paints, spray paints, or even chalk to make your planets bright and colorful. Then use fishing wire or thread to string each item from the ceiling.

● **Make a rocket...the sky's the limit!** Use large appliance boxes to create rockets that kids can actually enter. Fold *in* at the halfway point between each of the four sides of a box to create an octagonal "rocket." Cut a door and a few windows in the rocket, and then decorate the outside with white paint, flags, buttons, and stickers. Top it off with a pointy poster board "nose."

● **Let your imagination soar!** These ideas are just sparks to launch your creativity. Check out local resources—businesses, libraries, universities, craft and party-supply stores, and video-rental stores—for more ways to turn your facility into Space Mission Bible Camp.

Supplies: Everything You Need for a Successful Mission

Here are the supplies you'll need for each Training Station. These supply lists are also printed in their respective leader manuals. Note that some supplies can be shared among Training Stations.

 ## Sing & Play Blast Off

Things you can find around your home:
○ a Bible

Things you can find around your church:
○ a large color TV (optional)
○ a VCR (optional)
○ an audiocassette or CD player
○ a microphone/sound system
○ an overhead projector (optional)

Things you'll need to collect or purchase:
○ a robot costume, puppet, or prop (optional)
○ a *Sing & Play Blast Off Music Video** (optional)
○ a *Sing & Play Blast Off* audiocassette* or *Sing & Play Blast Off Music and Clip Art CD**
○ a *Space Mission Bible Camp Drama & Sound Effects* audiocassette (optional, from the Starter Kit)

Important Legal Information

For Your Information...

When you buy the *Sing & Play Blast Off* audiocassette, CD, or song lyrics transparencies, you also buy the right to use the thirteen Space Mission Bible Camp songs. You're welcome to play these songs as often as you like. But the companies that own these songs haven't given you (or us!) the right to duplicate any *Sing & Play Blast Off* products. Making your own copies—even to use at VBS—is against the law...a fact many people don't know.

○ the *Sing & Play Blast Off Lyrics Transparencies** (optional)
○ a space whistle* or another attention-getting signal

*These items are available from Group Publishing and your local Christian bookstore.

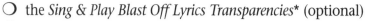

Bible Exploration

Things you can find around your home:

○ a Bible
○ paper grocery bags (two hundred to three hundred, depending on how high and wide you build your wall on Day 1)
○ newspapers
○ a card table
○ an audiocassette player
○ powerful flashlights
○ robes, sashes, head scarves, and sandals (for Hannah's and Peninnah's costumes)
○ a basket with a handle
○ a dish towel
○ a quilt or a bedspread
○ safety pins
○ a robe, a towel, two neckties, and sandals (for Thomas' costume)
○ bits of straw or dried grass
○ a small scrap of white cloth
○ a grape
○ a small cube of bread
○ a thorn
○ a cotton ball soaked in vinegar
○ a small, round stone

Things you can find around your church:

○ a wide-tipped black marker
○ a table
○ an index card
○ scissors

Things you'll need to collect or buy:

○ clear packing tape
○ black landscaping plastic or garbage bags
○ duct tape
○ a baby doll and a baby blanket
○ yummy-looking treats such as decorated cookies
○ fish-shaped crackers
○ seven plastic, fillable Easter eggs
○ photocopies of "Hannah and Peninnah's Script" (from the leader manual)

Pilot Program Pointer

To collect grocery sacks, check with your local grocery stores. Many merchants will gladly donate as many bags as you need when they learn you need them for a church project. (You might also ask them to donate twist-ties!)

- ⭕ a photocopy of "Andrew's Script" (from the leader manual)
- ⭕ a photocopy of "Thomas' Script" (from the leader manual)
- ⭕ photocopies of the "You're Under Arrest!" script (from the leader manual)
- ⭕ *Space Mission Bible Camp Drama & Sound Effects* audiocassette (from the Starter Kit)
- ⭕ a sample Mission Logbook from the Elementary Student Book (from the Starter Kit)
- ⭕ a few Brite-Tites (from the Have-a-Blast Games Leader)
- ⭕ a Bible Exploration stamp*
- ⭕ an ink pad
- ⭕ a space whistle* or another attention-getting signal

*These items are available from Group Publishing and your local Christian bookstore.

Space Crafts

Things you can find around your home:
- ⭕ sharp adult scissors or an X-Acto knife

Things you can find around your church:
- ⭕ scissors (Fiskars for Kids work best)
- ⭕ rubber bands
- ⭕ markers
- ⭕ masking tape
- ⭕ pencils or pens
- ⭕ an audiocassette player (optional)

Things you'll need to collect or purchase:
- ⭕ clean, empty juice boxes and straws (from the Mission Munchies Leader)
- ⭕ plastic cups
- ⭕ black electrical tape
- ⭕ transparent tape
- ⭕ one-gallon resealable plastic bags (thirty official Operation Kid-to-Kid bags are in the Starter Kit)
- ⭕ the Operation Kid-to-Kid information packet (from the Starter Kit)
- ⭕ a Space Crafts stamp*
- ⭕ an ink pad
- ⭕ "Operation Kid-to-Kid" posters*
- ⭕ a *Sing & Play Blast Off* audiocassette* (optional)
- ⭕ space lace*
- ⭕ Blast Off Rocket Kits*
- ⭕ Space Mission sticker sheets*
- ⭕ Talkie Tapes strips*
- ⭕ Tube-a-loon Rocket Kits*
- ⭕ a space whistle* or another attention-getting device

*These items are available from Group Publishing and your local Christian bookstore.

Mission Munchies

Food Supplies

	Item	Required Amount	Total Number of Participants		Total Required Amount
DAY 1	chocolate pudding	½ cup per participant	× _____	=	_____
	chocolate sandwich cookies	1 per participant	× _____	=	_____
	gummy worms	1 per participant	× _____	=	_____
	water	2 quarts for every 10 participants	# ÷ 10 = _____	× 2 =	_____
DAY 2	apples	3 per Flight Crew	× _____	=	_____
	peanut butter	2 tablespoons per participant	× _____	=	_____
	mini-marshmallows	3 or 4 per participant	× _____	=	_____
	M&M's candies	2 per participant	× _____	=	_____
	juice	2 quarts for every 10 participants	# ÷ 10 = _____	× 2 =	_____
DAY 3	popped popcorn	½ cup per *elementary* participant	× _____	=	_____
	unshelled peanuts	5 per *elementary* participant	× _____	=	_____
	raisins	10 per 2 *preschool* participants	× _____	=	_____
	Goldfish crackers	½ cup per 2 *preschool* participants	× _____	=	_____
	juice boxes	1 per participant	× _____	=	_____
DAY 4	Town House crackers	4 per participant	× _____	=	_____
	white frosting	2 tablespoons per participant	× _____	=	_____
	gummy worms	2 per participant	× _____	=	_____
	colored sprinkles				1 jar per Mission Munchies Service Crew
	food coloring (assorted colors)			=	1 kit
	water	2 quarts for every 10 participants	# ÷ 10 = _____	× 2 =	_____
DAY 5	peanut butter	2 tablespoons per participant	× _____	=	_____
	raisins	¼ cup per participant	× _____	=	_____
	teddy bear-shaped cookies	2 per participant	× _____	=	_____
	graham crackers	1 per participant	_____	=	_____
	juice or punch	2 quarts for every 10 participants	# ÷ 10 = _____	× 2 =	_____

· Serving Supplies

Item	Required Amount	Total Number of Participants	Total Required Amount
paper cups	4 per participant	× _____	= _____
clear plastic cups	1 per participant	× _____	= _____
napkins	5 per participant	× _____	= _____
plastic knives	2 per Mission Munchies Service Crew	× _____	= _____
plastic spoons	1 per participant	× _____	= _____
paring knives	1 per Mission Munchies Service Crew	× _____	= _____
resealable plastic bags (large size)	4 per Mission Munchies Service Crew	× _____	= _____
resealable plastic bags (sandwich size)	4 per Mission Munchies Service Crew	× _____	= _____
"snackmaker" gloves	3 gloves per participant	× _____	= _____
wire twist-ties	1 per participant	× _____	= _____
paper bowls	2 per Mission Munchies Service Crew	× _____	= _____
paper plates	3 per participant	× _____	= _____
paper grocery sacks	1 per Mission Munchies Service Crew	× _____	= _____
serving bowls	2 per Mission Munchies Service Crew	× _____	= _____
pitchers	2 for every 10 participants	× _____	= _____

 Other Supplies

Things you can find around your church:
- ○ antibacterial soap or individually wrapped hand-wipes
- ○ two or three rolls of paper towels

Things you'll need to collect or purchase:
- ○ an ink pad
- ○ a Mission Munchies Service stamp*
- ○ a *Sing and Play Blast Off* audiocassette* (optional)
- ○ a chef's hat*
- ○ a space whistle* or another attention-getting signal

*These items are available from Group Publishing and your local Christian bookstore.

 Have-a-Blast Games

Things you can find around your home:
- ○ large shoes or snow boots (one pair per Flight Crew)
- ○ extra-large men's sweatshirts (one per Flight Crew)

- ○ a watch with a second hand
- ○ laundry baskets or boxes (one per Flight Crew)
- ○ buckets (one per Flight Crew)
- ○ paper grocery sacks (one per Flight Crew)
- ○ plastic bowls (one per Flight Crew)
- ○ a plastic hoop
- ○ a beach ball or foam ball
- ○ marbles (one per Flight Crew)

Things you can find around your church:
- ○ chairs
- ○ water
- ○ transparent tape
- ○ scissors (one pair)
- ○ an audiocassette or CD player

Things you'll need to collect or purchase:
- ○ water bottles (one per Flight Crew)
- ○ sturdy paper cups (one per Flight Crew, plus at least ten extra)
- ○ construction paper (two colors, at least one sheet per person)
- ○ small balloons (about fifteen per Flight Crew)
- ○ eight- or nine-inch balloons (one per person)
- ○ Alka-Seltzer tablets (one per person)
- ○ foam rockets (kids will bring these from Space Crafts)
- ○ *Sing & Play Blast Off* audiocassette or CD*
- ○ masking tape or theme barricade tape*
- ○ Brite-Tites (from the Starter Kit)
- ○ Have-a-Blast Games stamp*
- ○ an ink pad
- ○ a space whistle* or another attention-getting signal

*These items are available from Group Publishing and your local Christian bookstore.

🚀 chadder's Space Mission Theater

Things you can find around your home:
- ○ a clock or a watch

Things you can find around your church:
- ○ Bibles
- ○ a large color TV
- ○ a VCR
- ○ markers
- ○ tape
- ○ twenty or thirty sheets of plain or colored paper
- ○ an audiocassette player (optional)

Things you'll need to collect or purchase:

○ a flashlight for each Flight Crew
○ an ink pad
○ photocopies of the *Chadder's Space Mission Adventure* video information letter (from the leader manual)
○ an Elementary Student Book (from the Starter Kit)
○ the *Chadder's Space Mission Adventure* video*
○ a Chadder's Space Mission Theater stamp*
○ the *Sing & Play Blast Off* audiocassette* (optional)
○ a space whistle* or another attention-getting device

*These items are available from Group Publishing and your local Christian bookstore.

Mission Send-Off Show Time

Things you can find around your home:

○ a Bible
○ a clock or a watch
○ an electric hair dryer with a "cool" setting
○ a dinner roll
○ a basket
○ a white robe or a white blanket
○ markers
○ twenty-five balloons
○ yarn

Things you can find around your church:

○ a microphone (if there are more than forty kids or if you're using a large room)
○ masking tape
○ slides, a slide projector, and a screen (if you decide to do a slide show)
○ a table
○ a long sheet of butcher paper
○ an audiocassette or CD player

Things you'll need to collect or purchase:

○ a small bag of M&M's candy (or another treat) for each Flight Crew
○ several rolls of colorful crepe paper streamers (two rolls for each row of children)
○ poster board
○ two Show Time jumbo balloons*
○ one bottle of disappearing ink* per crew
○ the *Sing & Play Blast Off* audiocassette* or CD*
○ the *Space Mission Bible Camp Drama & Sound Effects* audiocassette (from the Starter Kit)
○ a space whistle* or another attention-getting device

*These items are available from Group Publishing and your local Christian bookstore.

 # Preschool Bible SpacePlace

Things you can find around your home:
- ○ a Bible
- ○ an empty plastic soda bottle
- ○ sliced fruit
- ○ flavored yogurt
- ○ paper or plastic bowls
- ○ a hair dryer
- ○ rice
- ○ paper grocery bags
- ○ resealable plastic bags
- ○ fold-top sandwich bags
- ○ white facial tissue
- ○ fabric scraps
- ○ a spoon
- ○ a cotton ball
- ○ a comb
- ○ a dish tub
- ○ water toys
- ○ an old blanket or sheet
- ○ masking tape
- ○ transparent tape
- ○ paper
- ○ crayons
- ○ scissors
- ○ glue sticks
- ○ double-stick tape
- ○ rubber bands
- ○ black markers
- ○ glue

Things you can find around your church:
- ○ an ink pad
- ○ a clear or white balloon
- ○ an audiocassette player
- ○ permanent markers
- ○ poster board
- ○ blocks
- ○ tacky craft glue
- ○ sidewalk chalk
- ○ bubble solution
- ○ bubble wands
- ○ a small ball

Things you'll need to collect or purchase:

◯ colored tissue paper
◯ craft sticks
◯ fish-shaped crackers
◯ metallic star garland
◯ paint-stirring sticks
◯ Brite-Tites (from the Starter Kit)
◯ Tube-a-loons*
◯ Space Mission Bible Camp name badges*
◯ a Preschool Bible SpacePlace stamp*
◯ an ink pad
◯ Space Mission sticker sheets*
◯ Preschool Student Books*
◯ space blankets*
◯ space lace*
◯ the Blast Off Rocket Kit (from the Starter Kit)
◯ a *Preschool Bible SpacePlace* audiocassette*
◯ a Chadder Chipmunk puppet* (optional)
◯ a space whistle* or another attention-getting device

*These items are available from Group Publishing and your local Christian bookstore.

Spaceship Tip

Your Space Mission Bible Camp Starter Kit includes about thirty-three Brite-Tites. The Have-a-Blast Games leader will need half of these for elementary games. If you'll have more than seventeen preschoolers, you can purchase more Brite-Tites from Group Publishing or your local Christian bookstore.

Daily Schedules

Each day when kids come to Space Mission Bible Camp, they'll visit seven Training Stations. All Flight Crews will visit Sing & Play Blast Off, Mission Munchies, and Mission Send-Off Show Time together. In between these activities, the remaining Training Stations will run simultaneously. Training Station Leaders will repeat their activities four times, with a different group of Flight Crews each time. When it's time for groups to move to a new Training Station, walk through Space Mission Bible Camp and blow your space whistle (or use some other attention-getting device). This will help kids, crew leaders, and station leaders stay on schedule.

After you've assigned kids to Flight Crews, you'll need to assign Flight Crews to groups. Each group will consist of one-fourth of the elementary-age Flight Crews at Space Mission Bible Camp. To eliminate confusion with Flight Crew numbers, use letters or colors to label these four groups.

For example, if you have sixty kids, you will end up with twelve Flight Crews of five kids. You will then assign the crews to larger groups in this way:

A—crews 1-3	C—crews 7-9
B—crews 4-6	D—crews 10-12

If you have 150 kids, you will end up with thirty Flight Crews of five kids. You will then assign the crews to larger groups in this way:

A—crews 1-7	C—crews 16-22
B—crews 8-15	D—crews 23-30

If you have more than 150 kids, set up double Training Stations for Have-a-Blast Games, Bible Exploration, Space Crafts, and Chadder's Space Mission Theater. For more information on running double Training Stations, see the diagram on page 23.

You'll notice on the "Daily Schedule and Announcements" pages (pp. 74-78) that groups visit the Training Stations in a different order each day. This schedule shift provides welcome variety for kids and allows a different group to perform Mission Munchies Service each day. Mission Munchies Service is extremely important to the crews, who get a chance to do a real-life mission of love.

Preschool children will keep the same schedule each day but will perform Mission Munchies Service on Day 1. Preschoolers will leave their room and join older kids for Sing & Play Blast Off and Mission Send-Off Show Time. They view each day's *Chadder's Space Mission Adventure* segment while older kids are enjoying Mission Munchies. All other preschool activities take place in or near the Preschool Bible SpacePlace room.

Pilot Program Pointer

We discovered that it's a good idea to arrange your Flight Crews so that you have at least one experienced adult crew leader in each lettered group. Adults can offer encouragement, leadership, or helpful advice to younger crew leaders.

Spaceship Tip

Everyone loves a joke, silly anecdote, or comical quote. Consider adding "smile-inducers" to your daily schedules—it's an easy way to create a smiling staff!

Use the sample morning and evening schedules (pp. 72-73) to plan your VBS times. Then fill in the times on the "Daily Schedule and Announcements: Day 1" (p. 74). Note any announcements you want to pass on to your staff; then photocopy and distribute the schedule. Don't forget to give copies to the Flight Crew Leaders! Each day before Space Mission Bible Camp, fill in the appropriate day's schedule with times and announcements.

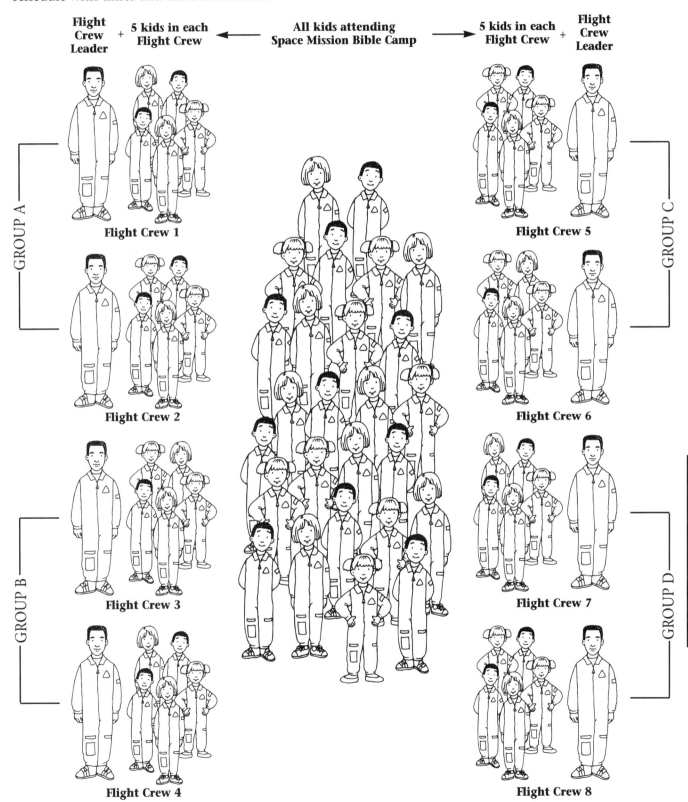

Flight Crew Leader + **5 kids in each Flight Crew** ⟵ **All kids attending Space Mission Bible Camp** ⟶ **5 kids in each Flight Crew** + **Flight Crew Leader**

GROUP A

Flight Crew 1

Flight Crew 2

GROUP B

Flight Crew 3

Flight Crew 4

GROUP C

Flight Crew 5

Flight Crew 6

GROUP D

Flight Crew 7

Flight Crew 8

Planning Your Space Mission Bible Camp

Sample
Space Mission Bible Camp
Morning Schedule (8:30-11:30)

Daily Schedule

Time	Group A Crews 1-5_____	Group B Crews 6-10_____	Group C Crews 11-15_____	Group D Crews 16-20_____	Preschool
8:30-8:45	Sing & Play Blast Off	Sing & Play Blast Off	Sing & Play Blast Off	Sing & Play Blast Off	Preschool Bible SpacePlace
Allow five minutes to "blast off" to your next Training Station.					
8:50-9:15	Bible Exploration	Space Crafts	Have-a-Blast Games	Chadder's Space Mission Theater	Mission Munchies Service
Allow five minutes to "blast off" to your next Training Station.					
9:20-9:45	Space Crafts	Have-a-Blast Games	Chadder's Space Mission Theater	Bible Exploration	Preschool Bible SpacePlace
Allow five minutes to "blast off" to your next Training Station.					
9:50-10:05	Mission Munchies	Mission Munchies	Mission Munchies	Mission Munchies	Chadder's Space Mission Theater
Allow five minutes to "blast off" to your next Training Station.					
10:10-10:35	Have-a-Blast Games	Chadder's Space Mission Theater	Bible Exploration	Space Crafts	Preschool Bible SpacePlace
Allow five minutes to "blast off" to your next Training Station.					
10:40-11:05	Chadder's Space Mission Theater	Bible Exploration	Space Crafts	Have-a-Blast Games	Preschool Bible SpacePlace
Allow five minutes to "blast off" to your next Training Station.					
11:10-11:30	Mission Send-Off Show Time	Mission Send-Off Show Time	Mission Send-Off Show Time	Mission Send-Off Show Time	Mission Send-Off Show Time

Sample
Space Mission Bible Camp
Evening Schedule (6:30-9:10)*

Daily Schedule

Time	Group A Crews 1-5	Group B Crews 6-10	Group C Crews 11-15	Group D Crews 16-20	Preschool
6:30-8:45	Sing & Play Blast Off	Sing & Play Blast Off	Sing & Play Blast Off	Sing & Play Blast Off	Preschool Bible SpacePlace
Allow five minutes to "blast off" to your next Training Station.					
6:50-7:10	Bible Exploration	Space Crafts	Have-a-Blast Games	Chadder's Space Mission Theater	Mission Munchies Service
Allow five minutes to "blast off" to your next Training Station.					
7:15-7:35	Space Crafts	Have-a-Blast Games	Chadder's Space Mission Theater	Bible Exploration	Preschool Bible SpacePlace
Allow five minutes to "blast off" to your next Training Station.					
7:40-7:55	Mission Munchies	Mission Munchies	Mission Munchies	Mission Munchies	Chadder's Space Mission Theater
Allow five minutes to "blast off" to your next Training Station.					
8:00-8:20	Have-a-Blast Games	Chadder's Space Mission Theater	Bible Exploration	Space Crafts	Preschool Bible SpacePlace
Allow five minutes to "blast off" to your next Training Station.					
8:25-8:45	Chadder's Space Mission Theater	Bible Exploration	Space Crafts	Have-a-Blast Games	Preschool Bible SpacePlace
Allow five minutes to "blast off" to your next Training Station.					
8:50-9:10	Mission Send-Off Show Time	Mission Send-Off Show Time	Mission Send-Off Show Time	Mission Send-Off Show Time	Mission Send-Off Show Time

*Kids will need at *least* twenty minutes to complete each Training Station. If you need to end your program promptly at 9 p.m., shorten your "blast off" time to two or three minutes between each Training Station.

Day 1

★ God helps us to be kind.

Daily Schedule and
Announcements

"Be kind and compassionate to one another, forgiving each
other, just as in Christ God forgave you" (Ephesians 4:32).

Time	Group A Crews_____	Group B Crews_____	Group C Crews_____	Group D Crews_____	Preschool
	Sing & Play Blast Off	Sing & Play Blast Off	Sing & Play Blast Off	Sing & Play Blast Off	Preschool Bible SpacePlace
	Allow five minutes to "blast off" to your next Training Station.				
	Bible Exploration	Space Crafts	Have-a-Blast Games	Chadder's Space Mission Theater	Mission Munchies Service
	Allow five minutes to "blast off" to your next Training Station.				
	Space Crafts	Have-a-Blast Games	Chadder's Space Mission Theater	Bible Exploration	Preschool Bible SpacePlace
	Allow five minutes to "blast off" to your next Training Station.				
	Mission Munchies	Mission Munchies	Mission Munchies	Mission Munchies	Chadder's Space Mission Theater
	Allow five minutes to "blast off" to your next Training Station.				
	Have-a-Blast Games	Chadder's Space Mission Theater	Bible Exploration	Space Crafts	Preschool Bible SpacePlace
	Allow five minutes to "blast off" to your next Training Station.				
	Chadder's Space Mission Theater	Bible Exploration	Space Crafts	Have-a-Blast Games	Preschool Bible SpacePlace
	Allow five minutes to "blast off" to your next Training Station.				
	Mission Send-Off Show Time	Mission Send-Off Show Time	Mission Send-Off Show Time	Mission Send-Off Show Time	Mission Send-Off Show Time

Today's announcements:

Planning Your Space
Mission Bible Camp

Day 2

⭐ **God helps us to be thankful.**

Daily Schedule and Announcements

"Give thanks to the Lord, for he is good; his love endures forever" (Psalm 107:1).

Time	Group A Crews_____	Group B Crews_____	Group C Crews_____	Group D Crews_____	Preschool
	Sing & Play Blast Off	Sing & Play Blast Off	Sing & Play Blast Off	Sing & Play Blast Off	Sing & Play Blast Off
Allow five minutes to "blast off" to your next Training Station.					
	Bible Exploration	Space Crafts	Mission Munchies Service	Chadder's Space Mission Theater	Preschool Bible SpacePlace
Allow five minutes to "blast off" to your next Training Station.					
	Space Crafts	Have-a-Blast Games	Chadder's Space Mission Theater	Bible Exploration	Preschool Bible SpacePlace
Allow five minutes to "blast off" to your next Training Station.					
	Mission Munchies	Mission Munchies	Mission Munchies	Mission Munchies	Chadder's Space Mission Theater
Allow five minutes to "blast off" to your next Training Station.					
	Have-a-Blast Games	Chadder's Space Mission Theater	Bible Exploration	Space Crafts	Preschool Bible SpacePlace
Allow five minutes to "blast off" to your next Training Station.					
	Chadder's Space Mission Theater	Bible Exploration	Space Crafts	Have-a-Blast Games	Preschool Bible SpacePlace
Allow five minutes to "blast off" to your next Training Station.					
	Mission Send-Off Show Time	Mission Send-Off Show Time	Mission Send-Off Show Time	Mission Send-Off Show Time	Mission Send-Off Show Time

Today's announcements:

Planning Your Space Mission Bible Camp

Day 3

⭐ God helps us to be helpful.

Daily Schedule and Announcements

"Serve one another in love" (Galatians 5:13b).

Time	Group B Crews_____	Group C Crews_____	Group D Crews_____	Group A Crews_____	Preschool
	Sing & Play Blast Off	Sing & Play Blast Off	Sing & Play Blast Off	Sing & Play Blast Off	Sing & Play Blast Off
Allow five minutes to "blast off" to your next Training Station.					
	Bible Exploration	Space Crafts	Mission Munchies Service	Chadder's Space Mission Theater	Preschool Bible SpacePlace
Allow five minutes to "blast off" to your next Training Station.					
	Space Crafts	Have-a-Blast Games	Chadder's Space Mission Theater	Bible Exploration	Preschool Bible SpacePlace
Allow five minutes to "blast off" to your next Training Station.					
	Mission Munchies	Mission Munchies	Mission Munchies	Mission Munchies	Chadder's Space Mission Theater
Allow five minutes to "blast off" to your next Training Station.					
	Have-a-Blast Games	Chadder's Space Mission Theater	Bible Exploration	Space Crafts	Preschool Bible SpacePlace
Allow five minutes to "blast off" to your next Training Station.					
	Chadder's Space Mission Theater	Bible Exploration	Space Crafts	Have-a-Blast Games	Preschool Bible SpacePlace
Allow five minutes to "blast off" to your next Training Station.					
	Mission Send-Off Show Time	Mission Send-Off Show Time	Mission Send-Off Show Time	Mission Send-Off Show Time	Mission Send-Off Show Time

Today's announcements:

Planning Your Space
Mission Bible Camp

76

Day 4

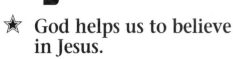

⭐ God helps us to believe in Jesus.

Daily Schedule and Announcements

"Believe in the Lord Jesus, and you will be saved" (Acts 16:31b).

Day 4 ⭐

Time	Group C Crews_____	Group D Crews_____	Group A Crews_____	Group B Crews_____	Preschool
	Sing & Play Blast Off	Sing & Play Blast Off	Sing & Play Blast Off	Sing & Play Blast Off	Sing & Play Blast Off
Allow five minutes to "blast off" to your next Training Station.					
	Bible Exploration	Space Crafts	Mission Munchies Service	Chadder's Space Mission Theater	Preschool Bible SpacePlace
Allow five minutes to "blast off" to your next Training Station.					
	Space Crafts	Have-a-Blast Games	Chadder's Space Mission Theater	Bible Exploration	Preschool Bible SpacePlace
Allow five minutes to "blast off" to your next Training Station.					
	Mission Munchies	Mission Munchies	Mission Munchies	Mission Munchies	Chadder's Space Mission Theater
Allow five minutes to "blast off" to your next Training Station.					
	Have-a-Blast Games	Chadder's Space Mission Theater	Bible Exploration	Space Crafts	Preschool Bible SpacePlace
Allow five minutes to "blast off" to your next Training Station.					
	Chadder's Space Mission Theater	Bible Exploration	Space Crafts	Have-a-Blast Games	Preschool Bible SpacePlace
Allow five minutes to "blast off" to your next Training Station.					
	Mission Send-Off Show Time	Mission Send-Off Show Time	Mission Send-Off Show Time	Mission Send-Off Show Time	Mission Send-Off Show Time

Today's announcements:

Planning Your Space Mission Bible Camp

Day 5

★ God helps us to be faithful.

Daily Schedule and Announcements

"Trust in the Lord with all your heart and lean not on your own understanding" (Proverbs 3:5).

Day 5 ★

Time	Group D Crews_____	Group A Crews_____	Group B Crews_____	Group C Crews_____	Preschool
	Sing & Play Blast Off	Sing & Play Blast Off	Sing & Play Blast Off	Sing & Play Blast Off	Sing & Play Blast Off
Allow five minutes to "blast off" to your next Training Station.					
	Bible Exploration	Space Crafts	Mission Munchies Service	Chadder's Space Mission Theater	Preschool Bible SpacePlace
Allow five minutes to "blast off" to your next Training Station.					
	Space Crafts	Have-a-Blast Games	Chadder's Space Mission Theater	Bible Exploration	Preschool Bible SpacePlace
Allow five minutes to "blast off" to your next Training Station.					
	Mission Munchies	Mission Munchies	Mission Munchies	Mission Munchies	Chadder's Space Mission Theater
Allow five minutes to "blast off" to your next Training Station.					
	Have-a-Blast Games	Chadder's Space Mission Theater	Bible Exploration	Space Crafts	Preschool Bible SpacePlace
Allow five minutes to "blast off" to your next Training Station.					
	Chadder's Space Mission Theater	Bible Exploration	Space Crafts	Have-a-Blast Games	Preschool Bible SpacePlace
Allow five minutes to "blast off" to your next Training Station.					
	Mission Send-Off Show Time	Mission Send-Off Show Time	Mission Send-Off Show Time	Mission Send-Off Show Time	Mission Send-Off Show Time

Today's announcements:

Recruitment

Calling All
Astronauts

Recruiting Training Station Leaders

Training Station Leaders are the backbone of your Space Mission Bible Camp staff. These are the people who will teach and show God's love to the kids who attend your program. Kids will look forward to seeing the Training Station Leaders each day—and so will you! You'll need at least eight volunteers—one leader for each of the following Training Stations:

- Sing & Play Blast Off
- Space Crafts
- Have-a-Blast Games
- Mission Munchies
- Bible Exploration
- Chadder's Space Mission Theater
- Mission Send-Off Show Time
- Preschool Bible SpacePlace

If you're expecting more than 150 kids to attend Space Mission Bible Camp, you may want to double up on Training Station Leaders. Purchase an additional leader manual for each Training Station, and run two sessions of each Training Station simultaneously. This will help keep Training Station group sizes manageable (fewer than thirty kids per session). Or have two Training Station Leaders team teach a large group of kids in a larger classroom.

Training Station Leaders should be adults or mature older teenagers. You'll find a specific job description for each Training Station Leader in the following pages. In general, you should look for Training Station Leaders who are...

- dependable church members or regular attendees,
- enthusiastic about working with children,
- excited about serving at Space Mission Bible Camp,
- patient and kind,
- good communicators,
- comfortable speaking in front of groups of thirty or more, and
- gifted in their Training Station areas.

Use the details in the following job descriptions to help you enlist leaders for the Training Stations. Give each leader a copy of his or her job description, and offer to address any questions or concerns that may arise. Invite Training Station Leaders and Flight Crew Leaders to your scheduled leader training.

Spaceship Tip

If you have enough volunteers, choose two people to team teach each Training Station, regardless of the size of your program. Training Station Leaders will benefit from a lighter load and an encouraging partner. Preschool Bible SpacePlace especially benefits from an extra set of helping hands!

Spaceship Tip

If you want to appoint an Assistant Mission Control Director, ask the Sing & Play Blast Off Leader or the Mission Send-Off Show Time Leader. Because these two leaders present their material only once each day, they'll be free to help you handle last-minute details.

List the names, addresses, and phone numbers of your Training Station Leaders in the chart below so you're able to quickly access the information.

Once you've enlisted your Training Station Leaders, you're ready to begin recruiting Flight Crew Leaders!

Training Station Leaders

Training Station		Leader's Name	Address	Phone Number	Other Notes
Sing & Play Blast Off					
Space Crafts					
Have-a-Blast Games					
Mission Munchies					
Bible Exploration					
Chadder's Space Mission Theater					
Mission Send-off Show Time					
Preschool Bible SpacePlace					

Recruitment

SPACE MISSION Bible Camp
Job Description

Sing & Play Blast Off Leader

Qualifications

You'll be a successful Sing & Play Blast Off Leader if you...
- love the Lord and love children,
- have experience leading songs or singing with children,
- can motivate and energize kids, and
- are comfortable speaking in front of large groups.

Responsibilities

As a Sing & Play Blast Off Leader, you'll be responsible for...
- attending scheduled leader training,
- repeating the daily Bible Point as you teach,
- learning the music and motions for thirteen Space Mission Bible Camp songs,
- teaching kids the words and motions to several songs each day,
- leading singing for the entire space camp,
- assisting with Mission Send-Off Show Time programs each day, and
- assisting the Mission Control Director as needed.

Related Interests

If you enjoy any of the following activities, you'll enjoy leading Sing & Play Blast Off:
- playing a musical instrument,
- directing or singing in your church choir,
- leading worship, and
- acting or drama.

Come help us launch kids on a mission of God's love!

Recruitment

SPACE MISSION Bible Camp
Job Description

Space Crafts Leader

Qualifications

You'll be a successful Space Crafts Leader if you...
- love the Lord and love children,
- are creative and fun-loving,
- can give clear directions to children, and
- show patience while working with lots of children.

Responsibilities

As a Space Crafts Leader, you'll be responsible for...
- attending scheduled leader training meetings,
- collecting necessary supplies,
- preparing sample crafts before Space Mission Bible Camp,
- explaining and encouraging children to carry out Operation Kid-to-Kid,
- repeating the daily Bible Point as you teach,
- helping children create one-of-a-kind crafts,
- leading four sessions of Space Crafts each day, and
- assisting with Mission Send-Off Show Time as needed.

Related Interests

If you enjoy any of the following activities, you'll enjoy leading Space Crafts:
- science projects,
- missions projects,
- arts and crafts, and
- working with your hands.

Come help us launch kids on a mission of God's love!

SPACE MISSION Bible Camp
Job Description

Have-a-Blast Games Leader

Qualifications

You'll be a successful Have-a-Blast Games Leader if you…
● love the Lord and love children;
● enjoy playing games;
● are positive, active, and energetic; and
● can organize and motivate children.

Responsibilities

As a Have-a-Blast Games Leader, you'll be responsible for…
● attending scheduled leader training,
● repeating the daily Bible Point as you teach,
● collecting necessary supplies for Have-a-Blast Games,
● clearly explaining each game,
● leading three sessions of Have-a-Blast Games each day,
● assisting with Mission Munchies Service each day, and
● assisting with Mission Send-Off Show Time as needed.

Related Interests

If you enjoy any of the following activities, you'll enjoy leading Have-a-Blast Games:
● team sports,
● outdoor recreational activities,
● cheerleading, and
● encouraging others to do their best.

come help us launch kids on a mission of God's love!

Recruitment

SPACE MISSION Bible Camp
Job Description

Mission Munchies Leader

Qualifications

You'll be a successful Mission Munchies Leader if you...

● love the Lord and love children,
● enjoy cooking and food preparation,
● believe children can accomplish big tasks,
● can give clear directions to children, and
● accept and encourage children's abilities.

Responsibilities

As a Mission Munchies Leader, you'll be responsible for...

● attending scheduled leader training,
● repeating the daily Bible Point as you teach,
● coordinating food supplies for each day's snack,
● setting up assembly lines to help kids prepare each day's snack,
● serving snacks to the entire Space Mission Bible Camp,
● cleaning up the Mission Munchies area after snacks are served, and
● assisting with Mission Send-Off Show Time as needed.

Related Interests

If you enjoy any of the following activities, you'll enjoy leading Mission Munchies:

● preparing and serving food,
● maintaining a clean environment,
● working in a kitchen or restaurant, and
● organizing and supervising teams of people.

come help us launch kids on a mission of God's love!

Recruitment

SPACE MISSION Bible Camp

Job Description

Bible Exploration Leader

Qualifications

You'll be a successful Bible Exploration Leader if you...

- love the Lord and love children;
- have a flair for drama and can play a role convincingly;
- relish a fast-paced, exciting atmosphere;
- believe in hands-on discovery as a learning technique; and
- feel comfortable facilitating group discussions.

Responsibilities

As a Bible Exploration Leader, you'll be responsible for...

- attending scheduled leader training,
- repeating the daily Bible Point as you teach,
- collecting necessary supplies,
- recruiting three to five volunteers to perform simple roles as Bible characters,
- setting up props for Bible Exploration adventures,
- leading four sessions of Bible Exploration each day,
- sharing props with the Mission Send-Off Show Time Leader, and
- assisting with Mission Send-Off Show Time as needed.

Related Interests

If you enjoy any of the following activities, you'll enjoy leading Bible Exploration:

- storytelling,
- acting or drama,
- leading discussions, and
- surprising others.

come help us launch kids on a mission of God's love!

Recruitment

SPACE MISSION Bible Camp
Job Description

Chadder's Space Mission Theater Leader

Qualifications

You'll be a successful Chadder's Space Mission Theater Leader if you...
- love the Lord and love children,
- know how to operate your church's TV and VCR,
- understand that videos can be effective learning tools for today's kids,
- enjoy facilitating group discussions, and
- ask questions to help kids connect the Bible Point they've learned in the *Chadder's Space Mission Adventure* video to their everyday lives.

Responsibilities

As a Chadder's Space Mission Theater Leader, you'll be responsible for...
- attending scheduled leader training,
- repeating the daily Bible Point as you teach,
- setting up a TV and VCR,
- cuing the *Chadder's Space Mission Adventure* video to each day's segment,
- helping Flight Crew Leaders facilitate group discussions,
- leading four sessions of Chadder's Space Mission Theater each day,
- showing the *Chadder's Space Mission Adventure* video segment to the preschoolers each day, and
- assisting with Mission Send-Off Show Time as needed.

Related Interests

If you enjoy any of the following activities, you'll enjoy leading Chadder's Space Mission Theater:
- watching movies,
- acting or drama,
- leading discussions, and
- operating electronic equipment.

Come help us launch kids on a mission of God's love!

88

Recruitment

SPACE MISSION Bible Camp
Job Description

Mission Send-Off Show Time Leader

Qualifications

You'll be a successful Mission Send-Off Show Time Leader if you…
- love the Lord and love children,
- enjoy being in front of people,
- are an expressive storyteller,
- like to laugh and have a good sense of humor, and
- can encourage and affirm kids' participation in each day's Mission Send-Off Show Time.

Responsibilities

As a Mission Send-Off Show Time Leader, you'll be responsible for…
- attending scheduled leader training,
- repeating the daily Bible Point as you teach,
- collecting necessary supplies,
- setting up props for each day's Mission Send-Off Show Time,
- practicing each day's Mission Send-Off Show Time script ahead of time,
- recruiting and training other Training Station Leaders to assist you,
- leading Mission Send-Off Show Time for the entire Space Mission Bible Camp each day, and
- assisting the Mission Control Director as needed.

Related Interests

If you enjoy any of the following activities, you'll enjoy leading Mission Send-Off Show Time:
- public speaking,
- acting or drama,
- storytelling,
- making people laugh, and
- supervising teams of people.

Come help us launch kids on a mission of God's love!

Recruitment

SPACE MISSION Bible Camp

Job Description

Preschool Bible SpacePlace Director

Qualifications

You'll be a successful Preschool Bible SpacePlace Director if you…
- love the Lord and love children,
- get down on the floor and interact with children at their eye level,
- use simple language that preschoolers can understand, and
- stock your room with blocks, dress-up clothes, modeling dough, and other age-appropriate toys and supplies.

Responsibilities

As a Preschool Bible SpacePlace Director, you'll be responsible for…
- attending scheduled leader training,
- repeating the daily Bible Point as you teach,
- collecting necessary supplies,
- leading a team of preschool Flight Crew Leaders,
- telling the daily Bible story in a fun and involving way,
- supervising preschoolers during outdoor activities, and
- leading preschoolers in singing.

Related Interests

If you enjoy any of the following activities, you'll enjoy leading Preschool Bible Space-Place:
- playing with young children,
- storytelling,
- singing, and
- being outdoors.

Come help us launch kids on a mission of God's love!

Recruitment

Enlisting Flight Crew Leaders

After you've enlisted Training Station Leaders, you'll need a group of Flight Crew Leaders. The Flight Crew Leader is an important part of each Flight Crew. Anyone in your church who loves the Lord and loves children can be a Flight Crew Leader! You'll need one Flight Crew Leader for every five elementary-age children.

Flight Crew Leaders don't have to prepare anything—they just come each day and join in the Space Mission Bible Camp fun. Their week will go smoother if you have a brief orientation meeting with your Flight Crew Leaders or if you invite them to your leader training meeting. The *Countdown!* video has special training information just for them. It gives them helpful hints on leading discussions and solving any problems that might arise among their crews. We've also included photocopiable handouts that orient Flight Crew Leaders with the teaching style at Space Mission Bible Camp and give them some ideas for capitalizing on extra time. You can find these handouts in the leader training section of this manual (pp. 111-116).

The following guidelines will help you find top-notch Flight Crew Leaders.

A Flight Crew Leader is...	A Flight Crew Leader isn't...
● a friend and a helper.	● the boss or the teacher.
● someone who offers kids choices.	● someone who makes all the decisions.
● someone who asks questions.	● someone who gives all the answers.
● someone who encourages kids.	● someone who yells at kids or puts them down.

Photocopy the "Mission: Be a Flight Crew Leader for Space Mission Bible Camp!" handout (p. 92), and post it in your church lobby. You'll be pleasantly surprised at how many Flight Crew Leaders join your team!

Spaceship Tip

If Flight Crew Leaders can't attend the leader training meeting, encourage them to watch the training video and review the handouts from pages 111-116.

Mission: Be a Flight Crew Leader for

SPACE MISSION Bible Camp™

Qualifications
- Be at least fourteen years old.
- Love the Lord.
- Love children.
- Like to have fun.

Responsibilities
- Attend a leader training meeting.
- Attend Space Mission Bible Camp each day.
- Participate in fun activities with a group of three to five elementary-age kids.

If you're interested, sign your name below or see

_____
Mission Control Director

today!

Name and phone number	Name and phone number
_____	_____
_____	_____
_____	_____
_____	_____
_____	_____
_____	_____

Recruitment

Enlisting Flight Crew Leaders for Preschoolers

Your youngest "astronauts" will need Flight Crew Leaders, too! Like Flight Crew Leaders for the elementary-age kids, Flight Crew Leaders for preschoolers don't need to prepare anything in advance. In fact, their job is even easier! Instead of leading Flight Crews, Flight Crew Leaders for preschoolers help their Flight Crews follow directions given by the Preschool Bible SpacePlace Director.

Flight Crew Leaders for preschoolers will play with children, help them complete art projects, and keep them together when they leave the room. To ensure adequate supervision for the preschoolers who attend your Space Mission Bible Camp, you'll need one Flight Crew Leader for every five preschool-age children.

What kind of person would make a good Flight Crew Leader for preschoolers?

A Flight Crew Leader for preschoolers is...
- a friend and a helper.
- someone who helps children complete activities.
- someone who gets down on the floor to interact with children.
- someone who encourages children.

A Flight Crew Leader for preschoolers isn't...
- the boss or the teacher.
- someone who completes children's activities for them.
- someone who supervises children from a distance.
- someone who yells at children or puts them down.

Photocopy the "Mission: Be a Flight Crew Leader for Preschoolers at Space Mission Bible Camp!" handout (p. 94), and post it in your church lobby. You'll be pleasantly surprised at how many Flight Crew Leaders for preschoolers join your team!

93

Mission: Be a Flight Crew Leader for Preschoolers for

Qualifications
- Be at least twelve years old.
- Love the Lord.
- Love children.
- Like to have fun.

Responsibilities
- Attend a leader training meeting.
- Attend Space Mission Bible Camp each day.
- Participate in fun activities with a group of three to five preschool-age children.

If you're interested, sign your name below or see

_____
Mission Control Director

today!

Name and phone number	Name and phone number
_____	_____
_____	_____
_____	_____
_____	_____
_____	_____
_____	_____

Recruitment

Enlisting Space Station Sign-In Personnel and Registrar

It's important to have staff near the registration tables to greet, welcome, and direct children. You'll also need at least one official Registrar to make sure registration goes smoothly.

For your Registrar, look for someone who...
- pays close attention to details,
- is organized,
- is familiar with many kids in your church (this helps when forming Flight Crews and provides kids with a familiar face on Day 1),
- understands the "combined-age" concept, and
- meets deadlines with a cheerful spirit.

Allow the Registrar to read through the registration section of this Mission Control Director Manual several weeks before Space Mission Bible Camp is set to blast off. Be sure that all registration forms and phone registrations are given to the Registrar.

For Space Station Sign-In volunteers, look for individuals who...
- are friendly and outgoing,
- are comfortable interacting with children,
- might enjoy playing the role of an astronaut or scientist, and
- want to help with Space Mission Bible Camp but can't commit much time.

You can have different Space Station Sign-In greeters each day—kids will love the surprise! Encourage your greeters to dress up in flight suits (even a plain pair of coveralls will work), robot costumes, or white lab coats. Greeters can direct children to Preschool Bible SpacePlace or can help kids find their Flight Crew Leaders.

Spaceship Tip

Be sure to have extra greeters on Day 1 since kids will need a little extra help finding their way.

Enlisting a Space Mission Bible Camp Photographer

Space Mission Bible Camp will be a memorable event—one you'll want to capture on film. With today's speedy photo processing, you can make photos a fun part of your Space Mission Bible Camp program.

Here's how:

1. Enlist a staff Photographer. This person could be...

- a parent,
- a church member,
- a friend or acquaintance from your community,
- the Sing & Play Blast Off Leader,
- the Mission Send-Off Show Time Leader,
- your pastor or another church staff person, or
- yourself.

Your Photographer should be familiar with the camera or video equipment he or she will be using.

2. Decide whether you want to shoot slides, prints, or video. The following ideas will help you decide how to incorporate photography into your VBS.

- **Mission Send-Off Show Time slide show**—Have your Photographer visit each Training Station and take slide photographs of kids in action. Take the slide film to be processed. On the last day of Mission Send-Off Show Time, show slides you've taken during the week. The Mission Send-Off Show Time Leader Manual suggests ways to incorporate the slide show on Day 5. If your Photographer is fast and if you have one-hour slide processing available, you can even have more than one slide show during the week.

- **Space Mission Bible Camp photo frames**—During Mission Munchies, have your Photographer take two print photos of each participant (including Flight Crew Leaders) and three print photos of each Flight Crew. (It may take two or three days to complete this project, so start early!) Have the print film processed, and then put the photos in cardboard photo frames to sell or give away as souvenirs. Photo frames with the Space Mission Bible Camp logo are available from Group Publishing and your local Christian bookstore.

- **Space Mission Bible Camp video night**—Have your Photographer videotape kids as they visit their Training Stations each day. Encourage the Photographer to interview kids about the things they're doing and what they like best. After your program, have a Space Mission Bible Camp video night where you show the video to kids, parents, and church members.

Pilot Program Pointer

When we took Flight Crew photos during our pilot program, the kids came up with a great idea. Several crews had worked before or after Space Mission Bible Camp to decorate their numbered Flight Crew sign, and they held up their colorful sign for their photo. Not only did the signs add a bright, personal touch to the picture, but they made it easy to figure out which Flight Crew was in the photo!

Recruitment

● **Space Mission Bible Camp photo display**—Have your Photographer take print photographs of kids in action. Then display the photographs on a poster or bulletin board in your church lobby. This is a great way to give church members a peek into Space Mission Bible Camp. And extra photos make great outreach tools as an excuse to visit new families who sent their children to Space Mission Bible Camp.

3. Meet with your Photographer before Space Mission Bible Camp. Talk about the number and kinds of photos you want. Decide who will have the film processed and who will select the photos or slides you'll use.

4. Watch kids' eyes light up as they see themselves in living color!

filling Out
Your Staff

In addition to Training Station Leaders, Flight Crew Leaders, a Photographer, and registration staff, you may want to enlist the following staff members:

● **publicity coordinator**—This person will be responsible for coordinating publicity before and during your Space Mission Bible Camp. This might include selecting publicity supplies, planning outreach publicity campaigns, inviting local TV or newspaper reporters, contacting church and community members, or arranging for community news releases. (TV coverage on Day 5 would be a super way to tell your community about Operation Kid-to-Kid!) The publicity section of this manual will help your publicity coordinator plan a great publicity campaign using the Space Mission Bible Camp publicity supplies available from Group Publishing and your local Christian bookstore.

● **family resource coordinator**—This person will be responsible for collecting the completed order forms (from the Student Books) and money for family resources, placing the order, and then distributing the items when they arrive. You may want to direct this person to the "Taking Home Space Mission Fun" section of this manual (pp. 152-154).

● **transportation coordinator**—This person will be responsible for coordinating transportation to and from Space Mission Bible Camp. This might include organizing car pools, planning van or bus routes, or actually picking up children and transporting them to your facility.

● **child-care coordinator**—This person will be responsible for providing or coordinating child care for the Space Mission Bible Camp staff. If possible, child care should be provided for all children (age three and younger) of Training Station Leaders and Flight Crew Leaders.

● **registration workers**—You'll need a team of four to five registration workers to ensure smooth, speedy check-in on Day 1. Registration workers will check in kids who have preregistered and will make sure walk-in participants complete registration forms. With your guidance, registration workers will also assign walk-in participants to Flight Crews. Plan to meet with the registration team *before* registration to go over the registration information on pages 143-144.

● **music accompanist**—If you want to use live music during Sing & Play Blast Off, you'll need to enlist a pianist, guitarist, or even a drummer to help lead singing.

When your staff is complete, you're ready to blast off!

Leader Training

Preparing Your Staff for a Space Blast!

Using the Countdown! Video

Welcome to Space Mission Bible Camp! We're glad you've chosen Space Mission Bible Camp for your church's VBS program. We know you're excited about Space Mission Bible Camp. The *Countdown!* video can help you get others in your church excited, too. The video is divided into two segments.

● **The promotional clip** gives a brief introduction to Group's Space Mission Bible Camp. In this five-minute segment, you'll discover what makes Space Mission Bible Camp different from other programs, and you'll learn how simple it is to turn your church into an astronaut training camp! Your church leaders, your Christian education board, and your congregation will see kids learning the Bible Points and Bible stories each day. Show the promotional clip in your children's church or Sunday school classes to get kids excited about their mission of God's love. (This is a great way to get most of your kids preregistered, too!) This short "teaser" will get everyone ready to blast off!

● **The overview and training portion** is a great tool for helping volunteers, parents, or other church members understand how Space Mission Bible Camp works. Your Training Station Leaders will be reassured to see kids successfully completing the activities described in their Training Station leader manuals. They'll see kids in a real Space Mission Bible Camp program enjoying Have-a-Blast Games, serving and tasting Mission Munchies, creating spectacular Space Crafts, and discovering Bible truths in new and meaningful ways. This segment, about twenty minutes long, will help Training Station Leaders see the "big picture" and become more confident with their roles.

This portion of the video also provides Flight Crew Leaders with valuable information about their role at Space Mission Bible Camp. Through interviews with real crew leaders from our pilot program, your volunteers will learn how to work with their Flight Crews, discover what's expected of them, and see the impact they can have on the kids at Space Mission Bible Camp. Flight Crew Leaders will even get tips on handling concerns or difficulties that might arise. Recruiting volunteers has never been simpler!

"Blast Off!" Leader Training Meeting

Pilot Program Pointer

To collect grocery sacks, check with your local grocery stores. Many merchants will gladly donate as many bags as you need when they learn you need them for a church project. (You might also ask them to donate twist-ties!)

You'll need the following supplies:

Things you can find around your home:
- a Bible
- two large plastic bowls
- two medium plastic bowls
- newspapers (a stack about one foot high)
- an audiocassette player
- two one-half-cup measuring cups
- a plastic garbage bag
- water

Things you can find around your church:
- a TV and a VCR
- chairs
- two tables
- paper cups (one per person)
- juice or water
- sheets of paper (one per person)
- pencils (one per person)
- six ink pads

Things you'll find in your Starter Kit:
- the *Countdown!* video
- the *Sing & Play Blast Off* audiocassette
- Brite-Tites
- the Blast Off Rocket Kit

- a sample Elementary Student Book
- the Space Mission Bible Camp leader manuals

Things you'll need to collect or purchase:
- popped popcorn
- twist-ties (one per person)
- unshelled peanuts
- hand-wipes (three per person)
- an Alka-Seltzer tablet
- paper grocery sacks (200 to 300 depending on the size of your room)
- photocopies of the "For Flight Crew Leaders Only" handouts on pages 111-116
- the *Sing & Play Blast Off Music Video** (optional)
- the *Chadder's Space Mission Adventure* video*
- the six Training Station stamps*
- snackmaker gloves*
- crew tote bags* (one per Flight Crew)
- a space whistle* or another attention-getting signal
- Space Mission Bible Camp staff T-shirts* (optional)
- Flight Crew Leader caps*

*These items are available from Group Publishing and your local Christian bookstore.

Spaceship Tip

Before your meeting, watch the *Countdown!* video. Note the places where you'll stop the video to invite teachers to try out actual Space Mission Bible Camp activities. If your VCR has a counter, you may even want to jot down the counter number of each stopping place in the margin of this manual.

Before the meeting, set up a TV and a VCR in your meeting room. Set up chairs facing the TV. In the back of the room, set up two tables. Then decorate your meeting room by hanging inflatable rockets, aluminum foil stars, or inflatable globes from the ceiling. To make your meeting room even more festive, try some of the decorating ideas beginning on page 58.

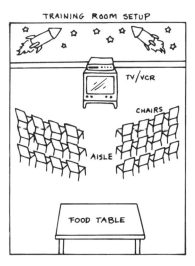

TRAINING ROOM SETUP

Pilot Program Pointer

We learned that it was a real timesaver to meet in the Bible Exploration station. With the leaders' help, building the "pit" was a snap!

Pour the unshelled peanuts into two medium plastic bowls. Place one bowl at the end of each table. Next to each bowl of peanuts, place a stack of snackmaker gloves. Then, next to each stack of gloves, place a large plastic bowl of popped popcorn and a one-half-cup measuring cup. Finally, place a stack of twist-ties next to each measuring cup.

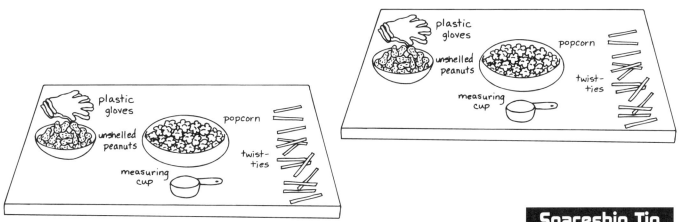

Create an informative packet for each of your Flight Crew Leaders to keep. Attach photocopies of the "For Flight Crew Leaders Only" handouts (pp. 111-116), and pass out the packets to your Flight Crew Leaders at the end of the meeting.

You'll need one Brite-Tite for every ten people. Tie the ends of each Brite-Tite together to form a loop. Set the Brite-Tite loops aside.

On each chair place a sheet of paper, six paper grocery sacks, three hand-wipes, a few newspapers, and a pencil. Play the *Sing & Play Blast Off Music Video* or the *Sing & Play Blast Off* audiocassette as volunteers arrive. Greet each Flight Crew Leader or Training Station Leader with a warm smile. Thank everyone for coming to this meeting and for helping with Space Mission Bible Camp.

When everyone has arrived, gradually turn down the volume of the *Sing & Play Blast Off* audiocassette, and then stop the cassette player. Blow your space whistle or use another attention-getting signal. Say: **Let's get ready to blast off to Space Mission Bible Camp! My name is** (name), **and I'll be your**

Spaceship Tip

The *Sing & Play Blast Off Music Video* lets volunteers see Sing & Play Blast Off fun in action! This video (available from Group Publishing and your local Christian bookstore) is a super way to add enthusiasm, build confidence, and teach all thirteen Space Mission Bible Camp songs.

Spaceship Tip

If you're providing attention-getting signals for your Training Station Leaders, this would be a good time to distribute them. You can use space whistles, available from Group Publishing and your local Christian bookstore, or any other noise-maker of your choice.

Pilot Program Pointer

The Flight Crew Leader caps were a simple way to visually set crew leaders apart from other helpers, "peeking" parents, or Training Station Leaders. Plus, many crew leaders used their caps as a name tag by writing their names on the bills of the caps. This turned out to be an easy way for kids to learn their leaders' names!

Mission Control Director. It's great to have each one of you as an important member of our Space Mission Bible Camp staff. Let's start our training time with a prayer.

Pray: **Dear God, thank you for the volunteers you've brought here today. Thank you for their willing hearts and their desire to see children love and follow you. Guide our time together, and help us remember the importance of each child in our program. In Jesus' name, amen.**

Say: **Today we're going to have some out-of-this-world fun together as we explore our Space Mission Bible Camp program. Our *Countdown!* video will give us a sneak peek at some Space Mission Bible Camp activities. But before we launch into our training, I'd like you to find a partner sitting near you and introduce yourself. Then trace your hand on the sheet of paper you found on your chair. At Space Mission Bible Camp, kids will learn that they can do anything with God's help. As you trace your hand, talk with your partner about why you decided to lend a hand this week. You have about thirty seconds to share.**

Allow time for partners to share. After thirty seconds, blow your space whistle to regain everyone's attention. Say: **This is my space whistle. I'll blow it whenever I need your attention. I'll also use it each day at Space Mission Bible Camp to let you know when it's time to dismiss your kids to their next Training Stations. You may want to use your own space whistle at Space Mission Bible Camp. Each day is packed so full of activities that you won't want to lose a minute!**

Say: **Would any of you be willing to share what you talked about with your partners? What made you decide to lend a hand this week?**

Take reports from several people, and then continue: **I guarantee you that Space Mission Bible Camp will be unlike any other program we've ever experienced! You'll be glad you helped out! Before we launch our *Countdown!* video, give everyone here a big...hand!** Hold up a paper hand, and show participants how to shake their papers to "applaud." Then say: **Let's begin our *Countdown!* video to find out why Space Mission Bible Camp will be unlike any other program we've experienced.**

Start the *Countdown!* video, and show the short promotional clip. Continue into the overview portion of the video.

After the host says, "Each child—no matter what age—contributes something valuable to the group," stop the VCR.

Say: **If you'll be a Flight Crew Leader at our Space Mission Bible Camp, please stand.**

Invite Flight Crew Leaders to introduce themselves; then have everyone give them a "hand" by shaking their paper hands. Say: **Without Flight Crew Leaders, Space Mission Bible Camp wouldn't get off the ground! We're looking forward to having a blast with you. To help you get a "head" start, I'm going to give you each a Flight Crew Leader cap to wear this week. Your caps will help kids, Training Station Leaders, and me find you more easily.** Give a Flight Crew Leader cap to each crew leader.

Continue the video. You'll hear the host talk about Training Stations.

After the host says, "You'll prepare just twenty-five minutes of material that you'll present up to four times each day as groups of children visit your Training Station," stop the VCR.

Say: **If you'll be a Training Station Leader at Space Mission Bible Camp, please stand up.**

Invite Training Station Leaders to introduce themselves and tell which Training Station they'll be leading. As Training Station Leaders introduce themselves, distribute the appropriate rubber stamps to the leaders of Mission Munchies, Have-a-Blast Games, Space Crafts, Chadder's Space Mission Theater, Bible Exploration, and Preschool Bible SpacePlace.

Say: **When children visit Mission Munchies, Have-a-Blast Games, Space Crafts, Chadder's Space Mission Theater, and Bible Exploration, they'll be excited to carry out the mission that's written in their Mission Logbooks.** Hold up a sample Mission Logbook from the Elementary Student Book, and point out the Training Station missions on the back. Say: **At the end of each session, you'll stamp each child's Mission Logbook to show that kids have accomplished their mission there.**

Have everyone give the Training Station Leaders a "hand" by shaking their paper hands. Say: **Without Training Station Leaders, Space Mission Bible Camp would be a "mission impossible." We're looking forward to having a blast with you.**

Continue the video. You'll hear the host explain how everything at Space Mission Bible Camp reinforces the Bible Point. Then you'll hear the host talk about Operation Kid-to-Kid.

Stop the VCR after the host says, "They'll discover that they can do something to really help others."

Say: **Not only will Operation Kid-to-Kid fill a need for children around the world, it'll show children right here in** (name of your community) **that they can accomplish great things through Christ. Turn to a partner and tell four *more* ways you think Operation Kid-to-Kid will** impact the children at our church. Each time you share a new idea, loosely crumple a sheet of newspaper and stuff it into a paper sack.

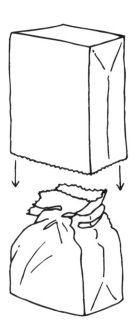

Allow a minute or two for partners to share ideas and fill their paper sacks. Blow your space whistle, and say: **Now crumple the top of your sack and pinch the edges together. Slip another paper sack over the top, and pull it all the way down to create a paper brick. As you make your brick, turn to another partner and tell one way you can help build enthusiasm for Operation Kid-to-Kid.**

After a minute, blow your space whistle, and have volunteers place their paper bricks under their chairs. Say: **Look at your hands. Just as the newspaper ink made an "impression" on your hands, Operation Kid-to-Kid will make a powerful impression on the kids here at Space Mission Bible Camp. Go ahead and use a hand-wipe to clean the ink off your hands.** While volunteers are wiping their hands, continue the video. You'll see children making snacks for the entire Space Mission Bible Camp.

When you hear the Mission Munchies Leader say, "They made the connection to service and to learning," stop the VCR.

Say: **Let's take a break and make one of the snacks kids will make at Mission Munchies Service. We'll make Helping Hands—a snack to remind kids on Day 3 that God helps us to be helpful. At Space Mission Bible Camp, Flight Crew Leaders help with snack preparation by handling sharp knives, pouring juice, and helping kids find jobs they do well. Let's have our Flight Crew Leaders be drink pourers.**

Training Station Leaders will work in an assembly line to make our treats. We'll need some helpers to push one peanut into each finger of the plastic gloves. Don't forget the thumb! Then other helpers will pour one-half cup of popcorn into the glove and push the popcorn down into the fingers. The next helpers will close off the glove by twisting a twist-tie at the wrist. When we've made a Helping Hand and a drink for each person, grab a treat and then find a seat near two other people.

When everyone is enjoying a snack, say: **Just as these plastic gloves are filled with good things, you'll fill children's hearts with the good** news of God's love. **Turn to a partner and tell him or her one way you can demonstrate God's love to a child this week.**

After a minute or two, blow your space whistle and allow a few volunteers to share their responses. Then say: **In Mark 9:36-37, Jesus talked about the importance of welcoming children.** From a Bible, read Mark 9:36-37: **"He took a little child and had him stand among them. Taking him in his arms, he said to them, 'Whoever welcomes one of these little children in my name welcomes me; and whoever welcomes me does not welcome me but the one who sent me.' "**

At Space Mission Bible Camp, remember that as you love these children, you're loving Christ, too! Let's continue our video and see the other ways we'll launch kids on a mission of God's love.

Continue the video. You'll hear about Have-a-Blast Games and how they help children remember the daily Point.

Stop the VCR when you hear the Have-a-Blast Games Leader say, "It goes real quickly and real smoothly."

Say: **Let's get up and work off that popcorn and juice by playing one of our Have-a-Blast Games! At Space Mission Bible Camp, even the games help kids discover God's love! Find about nine other people, form a circle, and join hands.**

When everyone is in a group and group members have joined hands, give each group a Brite-Tite loop. Have two participants join hands through their loop. Say: **In this game, you'll try to pass the loop around your circle without letting go of the hands you're holding. Ready, go!**

Give groups about two to three minutes to complete the task; then have them sit down. Ask:

● **What was it like to pass the loop?**
● **What did you discover about this game?**

Say: **When kids work together at Have-a-Blast Games, they learn that there's no such thing as a mission impossible. Let's learn more about Space Mission Bible Camp with our *Countdown!* video.**

Continue the *Countdown!* video, and watch as children explore exciting Bible adventures during Bible Exploration.

Stop the VCR when you hear the host say, "If Training Station Leaders and Flight Crew Leaders appear to be having fun and getting into it, the kids will follow your lead."

Say: **Participating in each activity is a great way to encourage kids to join in the fun, too. Turn to a partner and tell four ways you can participate during Space Mission Bible Camp. For example, you could sing and do motions at Sing & Play Blast Off or respond to questions during Bible Exploration. Each time you share, crumple a sheet of newspaper and stuff it into a paper sack.**

Allow two minutes for partners to share, and then say: **I'd like to hear some of the ideas you came up with.** Allow several people to share; then say: **Pinch the top of your bag together, and slip another paper sack over the top to create another paper brick. Remember, when you jump in and participate at Space Mission Bible Camp, you're building enthusiasm for our program!**

When everyone has made a second paper brick and has set it aside, say: **Look at your hands again. Sometimes, getting involved can be messy or a bit uncomfortable. As you use another hand-wipe to clean your hands, say a silent prayer. Ask God to give you the courage and energy to participate wholeheartedly in each day's program.** Pause for thirty seconds of silent prayer; then say: **Now let's return to our video to see what else is in store for us at Space Mission Bible Camp.**

Continue the video. You'll hear how fun and easy it is to lead Sing & Play Blast Off as well as the exciting dramas at the closing show, Mission Send-Off Show Time.

Stop the VCR after you hear the host say, "Again, an enthusiastic leader makes the closing show a meaningful time for all and a great way to wrap up the day."

Spread a plastic garbage bag on the floor. Say: **Our program's theme song this year is "Little Bit of Love."** Hold up a Blast Off Rocket. **This Blast Off Rocket reminds me of our theme song because just as a little bit of love goes a long, long way, this little bit of rocket fuel** (hold up a one-fourth piece of the Alka-Seltzer tablet; then place it in the rocket "booster") **will make the rocket go a long, long way.** Fill the rocket booster halfway with water, quickly snap on the lid, and place the rocket on the plastic bag. In a moment, the rocket will blast off!

Say: **Space Mission Bible Camp is full of surprising, exciting ways to launch kids on a mission of God's love! Life at Space Mission Bible Camp is never dull! Let's continue with our video to see what other** fun surprises are in store for us!

Continue the video to see and hear more about Space Crafts such as the Blast Off Rocket. Then you'll hear about Chadder's Space Mission Theater and will learn how preschoolers will be involved at Space Mission Bible Camp.

Stop the VCR after you hear the host say, "Preschoolers even learn about serving others by preparing snacks for the entire VBS."

Say: **As you can tell, everyone is on the move at Space Mission Bible Camp! So children (and Flight Crew Leaders) will enjoy some downtime while they watch *Chadder's Space Mission Adventure*. Let's have a little preview of one of Chadder's adventures.**

Play the first five minutes of the *Chadder's Space Mission Adventure* video to give everyone a taste of what's in store. Then stop the VCR, eject the cassette, and give it to the Chadder's Space Mission Theater Leader. Say: **Chadder has an amazing way of reaching everyone—from preschoolers to elementary kids—and helping them to apply the Bible Point to everyday life.**

Hold up a paper-sack brick, and say: **The Training Stations you've just seen will be important building blocks to children's faith this week. But without all of your help, our mission couldn't get off the ground! Use your paper hands to give yourselves a "hand."**

Pause while volunteers "applaud." Then say: **Flight Crew Leaders, we're especially glad for your help. You'll have a closer relationship with kids, and that can really help build their faith. You'll find that being a Flight Crew Leader is great, but you may experience a little turbulence on occasion. Get together with a person who's sitting near you. Think of four problems that might arise during the week. As you mention each concern, loosely crumple a sheet of newspaper and stuff it into a paper sack.**

After a minute, say: **Now take another paper sack, open it up, and stuff the open ends together to form another paper-sack brick.**

After a few seconds, say: **Let's cover our concerns with prayer. As we pray, use a hand-wipe to wash your hands. Remember that God can take away our fears and concerns.**

Pray: **Dear God, we know that some struggles may arise as we work with children who have many different backgrounds, temperaments, and personalities. Please take these frustrations and turn them into building blocks through which children can learn more about you. Amen.**

Say: **Set your paper-sack brick aside with the other two bricks. Let's see what special information our *Countdown!* video has for Flight Crew Leaders.**

Continue the video. You'll hear about what a Flight Crew Leader is and isn't, and hear how Flight Crew Leaders in a real Space Mission Bible Camp program solved difficulties within their Flight Crews. When the tape is over, stop the VCR.

Say: **Are you ready to blast off on our mission of God's love? As you prepare to meet the children in our program, remember Jesus' words in Mark 9:37: "Whoever welcomes one of these little children in my name welcomes me."**

Stack a few paper-sack bricks. Say: **This week, we'll be working together to build the faith of the kids who come to our Space Mission Bible Camp. Some kids may have a strong faith in Jesus, but...** *(knock over the blocks)* **others may be hearing about Jesus for the first time ever!**

We're going to work together to build a wall that kids will use during Bible Exploration. As you bring your bricks forward to build a wall, think of the ways God can use you to build the faith of the children in our program. When our wall is finished, we'll join hands and close in prayer.

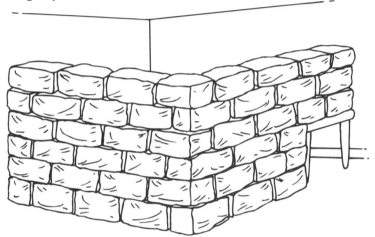

Follow the instructions on page 14 of the Bible Exploration Leader Manual to build a stable, secure wall. (If you don't have enough bricks, that's OK. Just ask a few volunteers to stick around afterward to make extra.) Then ask everyone to join hands, and pray: **Dear God, thank you for the opportunity to welcome children in your name. Show us how to build the faith of the children who come to our program. Help us show them that they can do anything through you. Please bless our time at VBS. In Jesus' name, amen.**
Let's get ready to have a blast!

Distribute the leader manuals to the Training Station Leaders, and Flight Crew Leader information packets and crew tote bags to Flight Crew Leaders as they leave. Remind Flight Crew Leaders to bring the tote bags and wear their caps to registration. If you purchased Space Mission Bible Camp staff T-shirts for your Training Station Leaders, hand them out with the leader manuals.

Spaceship Tip

You may want to photocopy the age-level information sheets (on page 24 of this manual and page 15 of the Preschool Bible SpacePlace Director Manual) to add to your Flight Crew Leader packets.

While your Space Mission Bible Camp crew is assembled, it's a good idea to take care of lots of "housekeeping" items. You might want to use the clip art on page 122 (or on the *Sing & Play Blast Off Music & Clip Art CD)* to create an "out-of-this-world" handout. Be sure to include the following:

❍ Tell your staff what time to arrive on the first day and where to meet.

❍ Distribute a map that shows where each Training Station will be (the *Sing & Play Blast Off Music & Clip Art CD* contains spectacular clip art to help you create a map).

❍ Inform Training Station Leaders and Flight Crew Leaders of procedures you'll follow if there's a fire or another emergency.

For Flight Crew Leaders Only

 ## What's a Flight Crew Leader?

If you've been asked to be a Flight Crew Leader, you've met two important qualifications: You love the Lord, and you love kids.

During Space Mission Bible Camp, you'll visit different Training Stations with a group of three to five kids. **You're not in charge of preparing or teaching activities—you just get to be there and enjoy them as part of your Flight Crew!**

The following guidelines will help you be a "far out" Flight Crew Leader!

A Flight Crew Leader is...	A Flight Crew Leader isn't...
● a friend and a helper.	● the boss or the teacher.
● someone who offers kids choices.	● someone who makes all the decisions.
● someone who asks questions.	● someone who gives all the answers.
● someone who encourages kids.	● someone who yells at kids or puts them down.

When talking with kids,

say...	don't say...
● let's keep moving so we can do as many fun activities as possible.	● stop talking and get back to work.
● listen carefully so you'll know what to do next.	● be quiet and listen!
● stay with the Flight Crew—we need your help in this activity!	● don't run around the room.
● that's a unique way of doing things! How did you think of that? Let's try it this way...	● you're doing it wrong!
● it's important that we all follow the instructions and work together as a team.	● don't do that!
● please move over here so you can see better.	● stay out of that area!

For Flight Crew Leaders Only

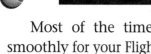

Most of the time, things will go really smoothly for your Flight Crew, but every once in a while, you may run into a dilemma. Here's some advice on how to handle different challenges.

If My Crew Won't Stay Together...

Encourage your Navigator to come up with creative ways to travel. Build excitement by saying, "Our Navigator came up with a really cool way to get to the next Training Station! Let's see if we can get there quickly while we do this."

Encourage Flight Crew spirit by working with your Cheerleader to come up with cheers to say as you travel.

If Older Kids Complain About Being With Younger Ones...

Highlight their helping role. Encourage them to help younger kids with crafts and other activities. Acknowledge them by telling younger kids, "(Name of older child) is really good at that. Why don't you ask him (or her) to help?"

If I Have a Clique in My Crew...

Cliques can make the Flight Crew experience unhappy for the outsiders. Encourage friendships between all crew members by pairing kids with partners they don't know very well during games and crafts.

If a Crew Member Won't Participate...

Help shy children feel welcome by calling them by name often and asking them questions directly. Respond to their questions with a smile and an encouraging statement such as "That's really interesting," or "Wow! I bet that made you feel special!" Also, try giving children special jobs. For example, assign them the task of finding a place for your crew to sit at each Training Station.

If someone doesn't want to participate in Have-a-Blast Games, that's OK. Space Mission Bible Camp can be tiring! Let children rest until they're ready to participate. Chances are, when kids see how much fun everyone else is having, they'll want to join in, too.

If People in My Crew Don't Get Along...

Quietly take the children aside. Tell them you've noticed they're not getting along. Let them know that although they don't have to be best friends, they do have to be together all week, so things will be a lot more fun if they can at least be kind to one another. (Use the daily Bible Points for these teachable moments!)

If I Have an Overly Active Child...

Pair this child up with yourself during partner activities, and suggest that he or she sit with you during quiet times. Try to make sitting still a game by saying, "Let's see how long you can sit still without interrupting. I'm timing you. Ready? Go!"

If the child is really uncontrollable, ask your director if you could have an Assistant Flight Crew Leader.

With a little patience and humor, you and your Flight Crew can have an "out-of-this-world" experience at Space Mission Bible Camp!

For Flight Crew Leaders Only

Who's Who in the Flight Crew?

During their first Sing & Play Blast Off session, kids will choose Flight Crew jobs and will place job stickers (from the Space Mission sticker sheets) on their name badges. Each child will have one of the jobs listed in the chart below.

● If your crew has fewer than five kids, some kids may have more than one job.

● If your crew has more than five kids, let kids share jobs.

● If children can't agree on who should perform each job, tell them that everyone will get a chance to do all the jobs. Assign kids jobs for Day 1; then rotate jobs each day so that by the end of the week, all children in the crew have had an opportunity to do each job. Kids can simply affix a different job sticker to their name badges each day.

Kids are excited about having special jobs! Encourage them to fulfill their roles, and provide lots of opportunities to do so.

Reader		● likes to read ● reads Bible passages aloud
Navigator		● likes to help others ● chooses action ideas for traveling between Training Stations (shuffling, skipping, hopping, galloping, or marching) ● serves as line leader to guide crew through daily schedule
Materials Manager		● likes to pass out and collect supplies ● carries Flight Crew tote bag ● passes out and collects Space Crafts materials ● passes out daily Mission Logbooks
Cheerleader		● likes to smile and make people happy ● makes sure people use kind words and actions ● leads group in cheering for others during Have-a-Blast Games
Prayer Person		● likes to pray and isn't afraid to pray aloud ● makes sure the crew takes time to pray each day ● leads or opens prayer times

For Flight Crew Leaders Only

What Do I Do at Each Training Station?

Sing & Play Blast Off is where kids will warm up for the day by singing upbeat action songs. Your job at Sing & Play Blast Off will be to...

● arrive a few minutes early;

● greet your crew members in your designated seating area;

● follow the motions and sing out loud; and

● remember that if you get involved, the kids will too!

Bible Exploration is where kids will hear the Bible story. Your job at Bible Exploration will be to...

● line up with your crew outside the door,

● ask how crew leaders should help out that day,

● keep your crew together until you receive other directions, and

● encourage crew members to participate.

Space Crafts is where kids will make cool crafts and learn about Operation Kid-to-Kid™. Your job at Space Crafts will be to...

● listen carefully to the instructions because you will most likely need to repeat them for some members of your crew,

● help kids make their crafts (*when* they need help),

● help crew members decide which school supplies they'll bring, and

● help clean up your area before leaving.

Have-a-Blast Games is where kids play team-building games. Your job at Have-a-Blast Games will be to...

● listen carefully to the instructions so you can help your crew members follow them,

● perform any tasks the games leader assigns to you,

● participate in each activity and cheer on your crew members as they participate!

Mission Munchies is where crews come for a tasty snack. Your job at Mission Munchies will be to...

● gather your crew in a designated area,

● quiet kids and help them focus on the Mission Munchies Leader as he or she explains the snack,

● talk with kids about their experiences at VBS that day, and

● help kids clean up your area before leaving.

Chadder's Space Mission Theater is where children will watch *Chadder's Space Mission Adventure*. Your job at Chadder's Space Mission Theater will be to...

● encourage kids to sit still and listen to the video,

● lead your crew in participating in the activities after the video, and

● lead kids in discussion when it's called for.

Mission Send-Off Show Time is an exciting review of the day's lesson. Your role at Mission Send-Off Show Time will be to...

● lead kids to your assigned seating area,

● participate in singing and other activities,

● remind your crew to participate without being rowdy or disruptive,

● make sure each child leaves with his or her craft and Mission Logbook, and

● collect kids' name badges as they leave and store them in your Flight Crew tote bag.

For Flight Crew Leaders for Preschoolers Only

What's a Flight Crew Leader for Preschoolers?

If you've been asked to be a Flight Crew Leader for preschoolers, you've met two important qualifications: You love the Lord, and you love kids.

During Space Mission Bible Camp, you'll visit different Training Stations with a group of three to five kids. **You're not in charge of preparing or teaching activities—you just get to be there and enjoy them as part of your Flight Crew!**

The following guidelines will help you be a "far out" Flight Crew Leader!

A Flight Crew Leader for preschoolers is...	A Flight Crew Leader for preschoolers isn't...
● a friend and helper.	● the boss or the teacher.
● someone who helps children complete activities.	● someone who completes children's activities for them.
● someone who gets down on the floor to interact with children.	● someone who supervises children from a distance.
● someone who encourages kids.	● someone who yells at kids or puts them down.

During Space Mission Bible Camp, you'll shepherd a group of up to five preschool children. Your role is to love, encourage, and enjoy the children in your crew. If you've never worked with preschoolers before, the following tips will help you.

● Learn the names of the children in your crew. Call children by name often.

● You'll have three-, four-, and five-year-olds in your Flight Crew. You'll probably notice big differences in motor skills (such as cutting and coloring) between older and younger children. Help children work at their own pace, and encourage five-year-olds to help younger children when possible.

● Look into preschoolers' eyes when you speak to them. You may need to kneel or sit on the floor to do this.

● Empower children by offering them choices. Ask, "Would you like to make a Tube-a-loon™ Rocket or play with blocks?" Don't ask, "What do you want to do?" or children may decide they want to do an activity that's unavailable or inappropriate.

For Flight Crew Leaders for Preschoolers Only

As a Flight Crew Leader for Preschoolers, You'll Be Expected to...

● arrive at least ten minutes early each day. Report to the Preschool Bible SpacePlace area (Day 1) or the Sing & Play Blast Off area (Days 2 through 5), and be ready to greet children who arrive early. Your welcoming presence will bring smiles to anxious faces!

● greet each child by name and with a warm smile. Help children put on their name badges each day.

● keep track of your crew members' Student Books. Store these in a Flight Crew tote bag, and place the tote bag in a convenient location in your classroom or church.

● sit with the children in your crew during group activities such as Blast Off Bible Story Time and Blast Off Sing-Along.

● accompany children to Blast Off Discovery Stations. Read the instructions at each station, and help children complete the activities. Distribute supplies from the children's books as needed.

● repeat the daily Bible Point often. The more children hear or say the Bible Point, the more likely they are to remember it and apply it to their lives.

● always check to make sure all children are accounted for before leaving the SpacePlace! Be sure children hold hands or a jump-rope as you travel.

● Never grab, pinch, or pull children as you travel. If a child lags behind, remind him or her to stay with the crew. You may want to walk behind your crew so you can keep all the children in view and avoid traveling too fast.

● report any potential discipline problems to the SpacePlace Director. He or she will help you handle problems appropriately.

● sit with your crew during Mission Send-Off Show Time. Help children participate in each day's show.

● collect children's name badges after each day's Mission Send-Off Show Time.

● release children only to a designated parent or caregiver. If an unfamiliar adult comes to pick up a child, refer the adult to the SpacePlace Director.

● assist the SpacePlace Director with cleanup and preparation for your next meeting.

Thanks for joining the Space Mission Bible Camp crew!

Publicity

Getting Your
Church and Community
on the Launch Pad

Launching SPACE MISSION Bible Camp in your church and community

You've planned, prepared, recruited, and trained. You've assembled an all-star staff for your Space Mission Bible Camp program. Now it's time to promote your program. Use the publicity items described below to get parents and kids in your church and your community to the launch pad for your Space Mission Bible Camp program.

In this section of your Mission Control Director Manual, you'll find the following resources:

● **Space Mission Bible Camp clip art**—Use the photocopiable clip art on page 122 to create your own custom promotional materials. You can make your own letterhead, memos, transparencies, and more!

● **Space Mission Bible Camp bulletin inserts**—Distribute information to everyone who attends your church. Just tear out the bulletin inserts on page 123, type in your church's information, photocopy the inserts, and slip the copies into your church bulletins. To help you conserve paper, we've included two bulletin inserts on a single page.

● **Space Mission Bible Camp table tent**—Photocopy the handout on page 124, and fold the page in half to use as a flier or bulletin insert. Kids can color the handout, cut out the rocket, and then push the rocket up to make it stand up on a table. These table tents will remind all family members of the fun that awaits them at Space Mission Bible Camp.

● **Invitation to parents**—Fill in your church's information; then photocopy and mail the parent letter on page 125. If you want to personalize the letter, make any desired changes, and then transfer the letter to your church's letterhead. You can mail the letter to parents in your church or your community.

● **News release**—Adapt the news release on page 126 to fit your church's program. Then submit typed, double-spaced copies to local newspapers, radio stations, and TV stations.

● **Community flier**—Photocopy the flier on page 127, and post copies in local libraries, restaurants, grocery stores, self-service laundries, parks, recreation centers, banks, shopping malls, and schools. Be sure to get permission before posting the fliers. You may also want to check with church members who own busi-

Spaceship Tip

Thanks to technology, you'll find much more clip art on the *Sing & Play Blast Off Music & Clip Art CD*. Use your computer expertise or involve a volunteer computer whiz to help you create dazzling publicity items.

nesses in your community. They may be willing to post fliers at their businesses—and they may even suggest additional business owners you can contact.

● **Publicity Skit**—Ask for volunteers to perform this skit (pp. 128-129)—a spoof on *Star Trek*—for your church congregation. The skit will give everyone a preview of the fun and excitement they can be a part of at Space Mission Bible Camp.

The following items are also available to help you publicize your Space Mission Bible Camp. Refer to your Space Mission Bible Camp catalog for illustrations and prices.

● *Countdown!* **video**—You may have already previewed this video when you examined your Space Mission Bible Camp Starter Kit. In addition to being a great leader training resource, *Countdown!* provides you with a "teaser" to show to your congregation. This short video clip gives church members a sneak peek at colorful Space Crafts, marvelous Mission Munchies, and exciting Bible learning that will take place at Space Mission Bible Camp! Plus the video explains more about Operation Kid-to-Kid, the exciting mission project your kids will take part in.

● **Space Mission Bible Camp staff T-shirts**—Invite Space Mission Bible Camp staff members to wear Space Mission Bible Camp staff T-shirts to church events in the weeks preceding your program.

You may also want to purchase a few children's theme T-shirts or iron-on transfers ahead of time and encourage children to wear them at school or in their neighborhoods.

● *Sing & Play Blast Off* **audiocassette or CD**—Get kids excited about Space Mission Bible Camp! Play Space Mission Bible Camp songs in your Sunday school classes or your other children's ministry programs.

● **Chadder Chipmunk plush puppet (large and small sizes)**—Invite this furry friend to visit your Sunday school classes—or even to make an appearance during adult worship. Chadder Chipmunk can announce the dates and times for your program. You can even ask Training Station Leaders to use Chadder to demonstrate Space Mission Bible Camp activities—Chadder tangled up in Brite-Tites...Chadder sampling Mission Munchies...Chadder trying to collect his Operation Kid-to-Kid items...the possibilities are as unlimited as your imagination!

● **Pattern for a full-size Chadder Chipmunk costume**—Ask a seamstress or tailor in your congregation to sew this larger-than-life Chadder costume. Then have a volunteer play Chadder all week long. Kids will love seeing their fuzzy friend before Sunday school, at midweek programs, or at other children's ministry events—and they'll be sure to register ASAP!

During Space Mission Bible Camp, be sure to have Chadder appear at registration, Sing & Play Blast Off, Mission Munchies, and especially at Preschool Bible SpacePlace!

● **Space Mission Bible Camp invitation postcards**—Kids won't soon forget this fun mask postcard that really gets them "into" their role! Send personalized invitations to all the families in your church and your community. Just fill in the time, date, and location of your Space Mission Bible Camp program, and drop these postcards in the mail—or hand them out at children's ministry events. These colorful postcards are available in packages of fifty.

● **Space Mission Bible Camp posters**—Hang these attractive posters on church or community bulletin boards to publicize your program. Be sure to include the name and phone number of someone people can call for more information.

If you're hanging a poster in your church, surround it with photographs from last year's program. When parents and kids remember the fun they had last year, they'll be eager to come back for even more Bible-learning fun at Space Mission Bible Camp.

● **Giant outdoor theme banner**—Announce Space Mission Bible Camp to your entire neighborhood by hanging this durable, weatherproof banner outside your church. If parents are looking for summer activities for their kids, they'll know right away that your church has a program to meet their needs.

● **Space Mission Bible Camp doorknob danglers**—Hand-deliver information about Space Mission Bible Camp to families in your community with these bright, lively doorknob danglers.

Choose the items you think will work best in your church and community. Then promote your Space Mission Bible Camp program until you're ready to blast off!

Space Mission Bible Camp
Clip Art

Launching Kids on a Mission of God's Love

SPACE MISSION Bible Camp™

Get ready to have a blast!

Join us for a week of unforgettable Bible-learning fun at Space Mission Bible Camp!

Launch site:

_____
(church name)

Mission length:

_____
(VBS dates)

Countdown begins at:

_____
(VBS starting time)

Reentry at:

_____
(VBS ending time)

For more information, call:

_____
(church phone number)

SPACE MISSION Bible Camp™

Get ready to have a blast!

Join us for a week of unforgettable Bible-learning fun at Space Mission Bible Camp!

Launch site:

_____
(church name)

Mission length:

_____
(VBS dates)

Countdown begins at:

_____
(VBS starting time)

Reentry at:

_____
(VBS ending time)

For more information, call:

_____
(church phone number)

Permission to photocopy this bulletin insert from Group's Space Mission Bible Camp: Mission Control Director Manual granted for local church use.
Copyright © Group Publishing, Inc., P.O. Box 481, Loveland, CO 80539.

Training Stations:

Your mission will include these

Get Ready to Blast Off

on a Space Adventure at

Publicity

Dear Parents:

Three...two...one...blast off! This summer,

_____ is launching an adventure of
(name of church)

cosmic proportions with **Space Mission Bible Camp.**

Each day your children will rocket into Bible learning they

can see...hear...touch...and even taste! Unique crafts, team-

building games, lively Bible songs, and healthy treats are just a

few of the **Space Mission Bible Camp** activities that will help launch

your kids on a mission of God's love. Children will also enjoy hands-on Bible

adventures and daily video visits from Chadder Chipmunk™! Your kids will even

participate in a hands-on mission project called Operation Kid-to-Kid.

Space Mission Bible Camp is great fun for chil-

dren of all ages; even teenagers will enjoy signing on as

"Flight Crew Leaders" who help younger children. And

parents, grandparents, and friends are invited to join

us each day at _____ for Mission Send-Off Show
(time you've scheduled your Mission Send-Off Show Time)

Time—a daily celebration of God's love you won't want to miss.

So mark _____ on your calendar. Countdown
(dates of your VBS)

starts at _____, and reentry is scheduled for _____.
(VBS starting time)   (VBS ending time)

Call _____ to register your children for a Bible-learning adven-
(church phone number)

ture they'll never forget.

Sincerely,

Your Space Mission Bible Camp
Mission Control Director

Publicity

News Release

Adapt the information in this news release to fit your church's Space Mission Bible Camp program. Then submit typed, double-spaced copies to your local newspapers, radio stations, and TV stations. You may want to check with them for any other specific requirements regarding news releases.

(Name of Church) Invites Children to Blast Off at Space Mission Bible Camp

"This year our church is reaching for the stars," says (your church pastor's name). "We're blasting off for Space Mission Bible Camp, where kids won't find any boring reminders of tedious schoolwork. Our Space Mission Bible Camp program will provide fun, memorable Bible-learning activities for kids of all ages. Each day kids will sing catchy songs, play teamwork-building games, nibble tasty treats from Mission Munchies, soar through Bible adventures, and create Space Crafts they'll take home and play with all summer long.

"Space Mission Bible Camp is a five-day mission of God's love. Kids will get to take part in a worldwide mission project that will reach needy children across the globe. We'll conclude each day with a festive Mission Send-Off Show Time program that gets everyone involved in celebrating what they've learned. Family members and friends are encouraged to join us daily for this special time. We hope Space Mission Bible Camp will launch our community on a mission of God's love."

Space Mission Bible Camp begins (VBS starting date) and continues through (VBS ending date). "Astronauts" will train at (name of church and church address) each day from (VBS starting time) until (VBS ending time). For information, call (church phone number).

Get Ready to Blast Off!

Join us as we launch Space Mission Bible Camp! You'll enjoy fun crafts and games, exciting daily shows, tasty snacks, lively music...and new friends!

Publicity

Launch Site:

_____

(church name and address)

Launch Date:

_____

(VBS dates)

Countdown begins at:

_____

(VBS starting time)

Reentry at:

_____

(VBS ending time)

For more information, call:

_____

(church phone number)

Publicity Skit

Have a few volunteers perform this skit before a worship service, during your announcements, at a midweek program, or during children's church or Sunday school.

Setting:
Your church. (That should be easy!)

Props:
You'll need a completed Tube-a-loon Rocket, a toy walkie-talkie, and a Space Mission Bible Camp flier (p. 127). Characters should dress in black pants and solid-colored, long-sleeved shirts (to look similar to characters from the first Star Trek television series). You may want to tape some kind of an insignia to the upper right-hand corner of the shirts. Mr. Shlock should wear some sort of silly ears—check a toy store or costume shop for ideas.

Captain Smirk and the Incredibly Shrinking Crew

Captain Smirk: *(Speaking into the walkie-talkie with characteristic drama and over-the-top intensity)* Captain's log, star date (today's date), 1998. We've arrived on planet Earth to investigate an astronaut training facility at (name of your church). It seems they're training children at something called *(looks at flier and reads)* Space Mission Bible Camp. Each of my crew members has been sent on a special mission to learn more about this...Space Mission Bible Camp.
(Mr. Shlock enters.)

Mr. Shlock: Captain, I've made a most interesting revelation.

Captain: *(Excitedly)* Mr. Shlock! You made it back alive! Quick! Tell me what's going on at Space Mission Bible Camp. Should we beam back to the ship immediately? Put up the deflector shields?

Shlock: Sir, I feel that we are completely safe and are in no danger of annihilation. This training program appears to provide an age-appropriate setting for juveniles to further their knowledge of scriptural texts.
(Captain looks at the audience with a puzzled expression.)

Captain: Huh?

Shlock: In other words, Captain, it is a fun place for kids to learn about the Bible. Why, the educators even use video reproductions of a gregarious rodent by the name of Chadder to further illuminate the scriptural texts in an enjoyable manner.

Captain: In English, Shlock!

Shlock: *(Sighs.)* Leaders even use a video about the adventures of Chadder Chipmunk as he learns how to carry out a mission of God's love.
(Spotty enters excitedly, waving a Tube-a-loon Rocket and speaking with a Scottish brogue.)

Spotty: Captain, sir! I've got to tell you about the Space Mission Bible Camp! I can't hold this much longer!

Captain: I knew it! They're manufacturing weapons to use against us! Set your phasers to "stun."

Spotty: No, sir! These aren't weapons! *(Tosses the Tube-a-loon Rocket into the audience.)* Ahh, I've wanted to do that since I picked this up at Space Crafts. That's where the wee ones go to create amazing arts-and-crafts projects! Isn't it wonderful, sir?

Captain: *(Pondering)* Space Crafts? *(Looks up.)* But wait, Spotty! Didn't Mr. ZuZu and Dr. Check-Out go with you? And the rest of the crew—were they abducted by Space Mission Bible Camp staff?

Spotty: No, sir. Mr. ZuZu saw the tantalizing treats in Mission Munchies and went for a snack. The others joined in Have-a-Blast Games. And Dr. Check-Out...well, the last I saw him, he was leadin' the music at Sing & Play Blast Off. *(Acts out motions from "Little Bit of Love" and sings a few lines.)*

Publicity

Captain: My entire crew has joined Space Mission Bible Camp? This is mutiny. This is a conspiracy. This is…

Shlock: *(Looks at his watch, and then interrupts.)* This is when the children traverse to Mission Send-Off Show Time, Captain. I believe that Flight Crew 7 is saving a seat for me. *(Gives strange hand signal.)* Catch you later. *(Shlock exits.)*

Captain: But Shlock!

Spotty: Aye, sir. And I've promised to help Dr. Check-Out lead singing, too. I'll beam up later. *(Spotty exits.)*

Captain: You too, Spotty? *(Pauses, and then pulls out walkie-talkie again.)* Captain's log, star date (today's date), 1998. My crew has abandoned me for the fun and excitement of Space Mission Bible Camp. As I consider the implications of this, I wonder…I wonder…what am I sitting here for? *(Runs offstage.)*

Registration

Welcoming
Your Astronauts

Making an
Unforgettable Impression

Space Mission Bible Camp is a fun place for kids to discover how God helps them accomplish anything. Once kids sample the activities at each Training Station, they'll want to "soar" with you all week long. But you can start generating excitement and enthusiasm for Space Mission Bible Camp before kids even set foot in a Training Station.

The excitement starts with preregistration. About a month before your scheduled Space Mission Bible Camp program, you'll begin preregistering children in your church. Preregistration is simple: Just make copies of the "Space Mission Bible Camp Registration Form" (p. 148), and have parents fill them out. Or slip Space Mission Bible Camp registration cards into your church bulletins. (These registration cards are available from Group Publishing and your local Christian bookstore.) Save the completed registration forms; you'll use them to assign Flight Crews (described on page 135).

To pique kids' (and parents') interest in preregistration, try incorporating some of the following activities:

● **Show the *Countdown!* promotional video clip in your church worship service.** This video clip gives everyone in your church a chance to preview Space Mission Bible Camp. It includes glimpses of each Space Mission Bible Camp Training Station so church members can see all the fun Bible learning that's packed into the Space Mission Bible Camp program.

● **Have kids in your children's ministry programs design their own Space Mission Bible Camp posters.** Check out books about space travel or space exploration from your local public library. Talk to kids about "space stuff" that interests them, such as spacewalks, pictures of Mars, shooting stars, and weightlessness. Let kids draw their own spacecraft or illustrate what they imagine other planets look like. Provide glitter, aluminum foil, or pieces of space blankets so kids can add sparkle to their pictures.

● **Have Sunday school classes work together to build Space Mission Bible Camp robots.** Provide three-dimensional materials such as cardboard boxes, paper towel tubes, empty soda containers, pie tins, silver dryer ducts, and garbage cans. Challenge classes to use the materials to make robots they can display in their classrooms. Kids who are attending Space Mission Bible Camp can sign their names or attach their photos on the finished robots. Training Station Leaders or other adults might also enjoy this project!

Registration

EXTRA IDEA!

If you want to launch your space program with extra style and pizazz, consider planning an all-church space and science fair. Decorate your fellowship hall, church lawn, or a nearby park, and set up one or more of the following "space stations."

● Use glittery face paints to create sun, star, or planet designs on kids' faces.

● Rent a "moonwalk" inflatable trampoline, and let kids (and adults) jump and hop as if they're walking in space. Or rent a gyroscope, and let adults feel the dizzying sensation of being weightless!

● Set out magnets and several metal objects so preschoolers can experiment with them.

● Provide glue, paint, and a variety of pasta shapes—such as lasagna, wheels, farfalle, or letters—and let kids design their own rockets and other aircraft.

● Have a paper-airplane-making contest. Contestants of all ages can compete for most unique design, longest flight, highest flight, or most interesting takeoff.

● Ask model-rocket enthusiasts to bring their rockets and stage a rocket launch for others to watch. Be sure to let everyone in on an exciting countdown!

● Provide dried fruit, jerky, star-shaped cookies, crescent rolls, and Tang (you may have to explain its significance to children!) at a snack area. You may even want to set out a tray of sugar cookies and let individuals decorate them to look like strange planets or stars.

● If it's a breezy day, set out a variety of kites, and let families create tails from fabric scraps or crepe paper streamers. Families can fly their kites in an open area.

● Set out marshmallows or colorful gumdrops and uncooked spaghetti. Let kids break the spaghetti into various lengths and then stick the ends into gumdrops to create constellations.

● Create a static experiment station. Set out balloons, and let individuals blow up a few balloons and tie them off. Then demonstrate how to rub the balloons on your hair or on a piece of wool and then place the balloons on a wall or other vertical surface. Kids will love watching the balloons "stick."

The excitement continues as kids arrive at Space Mission Bible Camp. At registration, remember that some families from your community are coming into contact with your church for the first time. You don't want their first impression to be of long, boring registration lines. To make an unforgettable impression, try the following ideas:

● **Prepare a large "Welcome, Astronauts!" sign, and post it behind your registration table.** Ask an artistic person in your church to write, "Welcome, Astronauts!" in large block letters on a large sheet of poster board or butcher paper. Decorate the sign with paints, markers, glitter, or confetti for a festive look.

● **Set up the Space Mission Bible Camp Starter Kit can as a display on your registration table.** Set the can on top of a silver space blanket for a real space-camp feel. You may want to fill the can with Starburst fruit chews and miniature Mars or Milky Way candy bars for kids to enjoy as they register.

● **Have the Have-a-Blast Games Leader (or someone else) toss around samples of the Follow-Me Comets that preschoolers will make during VBS.** Kids will enjoy watching the bright, shiny toys flying through the air. This will also give kids a chance to meet their games leader in a fun setting.

● **Play the *Sing & Play Blast Off* audiocassette or the *Sing & Play Blast Off Music Video.*** The fun, upbeat music will provide a fun, festive atmosphere.

● **Use a Chadder Chipmunk puppet (available from Group Publishing and your local Christian bookstore) to greet kids who are waiting in the registration line.** Younger children who might be afraid to leave their parents or caregivers will be reassured by this fuzzy friend—especially when they hear that they'll get to see him each day in the *Chadder's Space Mission Adventure* video. And if you've used Group's VBS in the past, children will delight in seeing Chadder—their familiar, furry friend!

● **Pass out sample Mission Munchies.** You can use a snack from the Mission Munchies Leader Manual or you can come up with your own. Be sure to include drinks—especially if the weather's hot.

Blast off for an unforgettable space mission!

Setting Up Flight Crews

One week before Space Mission Bible Camp begins, assign preregistered kids to Flight Crews. Participating in Flight Crews is an important part of kids' Space Mission Bible Camp experience, so use care and consideration when making Flight Crew assignments. Follow the guidelines given in the planning section of this manual under "One Week Before Space Mission Bible Camp" (p. 51) or the guidelines on the back of the "Signs and Planning" poster. If you don't know very many of the kids who will attend Space Mission Bible Camp, ask Sunday school teachers or other Christian education workers to help you assign kids to crews.

Step One: Inventory Your Registrations

● When you're ready to assign crews, make nine copies of the "Age-Level Roster" form (p. 145). Label the forms with grades K, 1, 2, 3, 4, and 5; do the same using "3-year-olds," "4-year-olds," and "5-year-olds" (for 5-year-olds who have not yet attended kindergarten). List the names of preregistered kids on the appropriate age-level rosters.

● Count how many kids have preregistered for your Space Mission Bible Camp, and divide them into two groups: elementary-age children and preschool-age children. Elementary-age children have completed kindergarten, fifth grade, or any grade in between. Be sure to check forms carefully—some families may have registered more than one child on one form. If children who have completed sixth grade want to participate in your program, that's OK; keep in mind, though, that most of the Space Mission Bible Camp activities are designed for slightly younger kids. Space Mission Bible Camp is designed to use young people in grades

Spaceship Tip

If you have a willing seamstress or tailor in your congregation, have him or her sew the life-size Chadder Chipmunk costume (pattern available from Group Publishing and your local Christian bookstore). Then ask a volunteer to play Chadder and greet children at registration. Chadder's antics and warmth will be the perfect start to Space Mission Bible Camp!

Registration

Spaceship Tip

Prayerfully consider the responsibility of setting up Flight Crews. These small groups have a powerful impact on children, helping them form special relationships and memories.

Registration

six and higher in leadership roles; encourage mature sixth-graders to serve as Flight Crew Leaders for preschoolers. For other ideas about how upper-elementary kids can participate in Space Mission Bible Camp, see page 26.

Step Two: Determine How Many Flight Crews You'll Have

● Each Flight Crew will have no more than five kids and one adult or teenage Flight Crew Leader. (Preschool crews may have a junior high leader.) Divide the total number of preregistered elementary-age kids by five to discover how many elementary Flight Crews you'll have. Do the same with preschool preregistrations. Use the line below to help you determine this.

If you want to encourage kids to bring their friends to Space Mission Bible Camp, you may want to place only three or four kids in each crew. This will allow you to add to your crews.

Once you've determined the number of preschool and elementary crews you'll need, check to see that you've recruited enough Flight Crew Leaders. Remember that you'll need a Flight Crew Leader for every crew, plus a few extra leaders on hand on Day 1.

Number of (elementary or preschool) kids _____ / at five kids per crew = Number of Flight Crews_____.

Step Three: Assign Flight Crews

● Photocopy the "Flight Crew Roster" form (p. 146). You'll need one form for every four Flight Crews.

● Assign a Flight Crew Leader to each Flight Crew. It's helpful to indicate whether the leader is an adult (A), a teenager (T), or junior higher (J).

● **Preschool Flight Crews**

Gather the age-level rosters for ages three, four, and five. Beginning with the three-year-old age-level roster, assign one child from each preschool age-level roster to each preschool Flight Crew. Since each crew has five spaces, you'll have more than one representative of some age levels in each crew. Remember, it's helpful to have a mixture of preschool ages in each crew so crew leaders can work with three-year-olds, while five-year-olds may be a bit more self-sufficient. Be sure to check off the names on the age-level rosters as you assign them to crews.

● **Elementary Flight Crews**

Gather the elementary age-level rosters. Beginning with the kindergarten age-level roster, assign one child from each age-level roster to each Flight Crew. Since each crew has only five spaces, you won't be able to have every age level in every crew. Check off the names on the age-level rosters as you assign them to crews. Refer to the examples on the next page for ways to spread age levels evenly among your Flight Crews.

You aren't *required* to group children in combined-age Flight Crews, but we strongly recommend it because it works so well. Children, young and old alike, help one another throughout their time together. Plus you'll minimize discipline problems because the diversity frees children from the need to compete with peers of the same age. For more information on the benefits of combining ages, see page 24.

If you have an equal number of children in each grade level...

● fill one-third of your crews with kids who have completed kindergarten and grades two through five.

● fill one-third of your crews with kids who have completed grades one through five.

● fill one-third of your crews with kids who have completed kindergarten through grade four.

If you have an abundance of younger children...

● group kindergartners, second-graders, third-graders, and fifth-graders together. Assign two kindergartners to each crew if necessary. Remind Flight Crew Leaders to encourage the fifth-graders to help younger children. Fifth-graders might even be named "Assistant Flight Crew Leaders."

● group kids in grades one through four together. Assign two first-graders to each crew if necessary.

If you have an abundance of older children...

● group kindergartners, first-graders, second-graders, and fourth-graders together. Assign two fourth graders to each crew if necessary.

● group grades two through five together. Assign two fifth-graders to each crew if necessary.

If you have fewer than five kids per Flight Crew...

● vary the age-level mix, if possible, so you'll have open spaces in your program at every age level. These spaces can be filled by kids who haven't preregistered.

Step Four: Complete the Master List

● Double-check to make sure you've assigned each participant to a Flight Crew. Then write kids' Flight Crew numbers on their registration forms next to their names.

● Alphabetize the registration forms, and then transfer kids' names and crew numbers to the "Alphabetical Master List" (p. 147). Put a "P" in the crew-number space next to each preschooler's name.

● Give the preschool registration forms, age-level rosters, and Flight Crew rosters to the Preschool Bible SpacePlace Director.

Bring the "Age-Level Roster" lists, "Flight Crew Roster" lists, and "Alphabetical Master List" with you to registration!

Let Flight Crew Leaders Help With Space Station Sign-In

Flight Crew Leaders can help you soar through registration! They'll meet and greet kids and will help keep kids busy while others are standing in line. Read on to find out how Flight Crew Leaders will help make registration a snap.

Flight Crew Leader Registration Supplies

Each Flight Crew Leader will need the following supplies:
- a permanent marker,
- colorful washable markers or posters,
- one sheet of poster board,
- a copy of the "Flight Crew Roster" for his or her crew, and
- masking tape.

If you didn't distribute Flight Crew name badges, one-yard lengths of glow-in-the-dark space lace, Student Books, Space Mission sticker sheets, and tote bags at your leader training meeting, you'll also need to give these supplies to each Flight Crew Leader. Each child will need a Student Book, a Space Mission sticker sheet, and a name badge strung on one yard of space lace.

Flight Crew Leader Registration Procedures

- Give each Flight Crew Leader a Space Mission Bible Camp cap to wear. This helps Training Station Leaders and kids recognize crew leaders.
- When Flight Crew Leaders arrive, they'll write their Flight Crew numbers on sheets of poster board then hang the number posters *where they can be seen easily* in the Sing & Play Blast Off area. It helps if they hang the posters in numerical order.
- After children complete the registration process, they'll meet their Flight Crew Leaders by their crew-number posters in Sing & Play Blast Off.
- Flight Crew Leaders will greet kids and welcome them to Space Mission Bible Camp. Leaders will use permanent markers to write kids' names and crew numbers on their name badges. If additional kids have been assigned to Flight Crews during registration, Flight Crew Leaders will update their copies of the "Flight Crew Roster."
- Flight Crews will work on decorating their crew-number sign while they wait for others to arrive. This is a fun time for Flight Crew Leaders and crew members to get acquainted.

Spaceship Tip

Having Flight Crew Leaders write kids' names on their name badges is a nice way for leaders to learn the names of their crew members.

Registration Day
Is Here!

Registration Supplies

For registration, you'll need the following items:

● entry decorations such as space blankets, balloons, white lights, paper stars, and cardboard "robots"

● three tables

● four signs:

✔ "Preregistered—kindergarten through fifth grade"

✔ "Walk-in registration—kindergarten through fifth grade"

✔ two "Preschool registration" signs with arrows pointing to the Preschool Bible SpacePlace

● two copies of each completed elementary "Flight Crew Roster" (p. 146)

● one copy of each completed preschool "Flight Crew Roster" (p. 146)

● three copies of each completed elementary "Age-Level Roster" (p. 145)

● two copies of each completed preschool "Age-Level Roster" (p. 145)

● two copies of the completed "Alphabetical Master List" (p. 147)

● plenty of pens and pencils

● at least five volunteers, including the Registrar

● chairs for your volunteers

● blank copies of the "Space Mission Bible Camp Registration Form" (p. 148).

Registration Setup

Before registration, set up two tables in your church's foyer or entry area. If weather permits, you may want to set up your tables outside to allow more room. (It's a good idea to place these tables far apart to avoid a bottleneck.) Put the "Preregistered—kindergarten through fifth grade" sign above one table. Put the "Walk-in registration—kindergarten through fifth grade" sign above the other table. Set up chairs for your volunteers at each table. Be sure to place your signs high enough for everyone to clearly see!

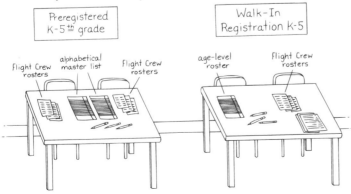

Spaceship Tip

You may want to give each Flight Crew Leader a few extra name badges and one-yard lengths of space lace for walk-in registrants who may join their crews.

Preregistered Table

On the table below the preregistered sign, place

- a copy of the completed "Alphabetical Master List" (p. 147),
- a copy of each completed "Flight Crew Roster" (p. 146), and
- several pencils.

Walk-In Registration Table

On the table below the walk-in registration sign, place

- a copy of each completed elementary "Age-Level Roster" (p. 145),
- a copy of each completed "Flight Crew Roster" (p. 146),
- copies of the "Registration Form" (p. 148), and
- several pens or pencils.

Take the Express Lane!

Consider an "Express Preregistered Check-In" system. Have a couple of volunteers stand at the entryway, holding copies of the "Alphabetical Master List." Kids who are preregistered can tell the "Express Checkers" their names and have the Checkers look at the list to see which Flight Crews kids are in. Or if you're low on volunteers, enlarge your "Alphabetical Master List" and post several copies of it in your registration area. Kids (and parents) can check the list to find what Flight Crews they're on and then simply find their crew numbers and Flight Crew Leaders!

Preschool Registration Table

Set up a table (or several if you have more than twenty-five preschoolers) outside your Preschool Bible SpacePlace area. Put the two "Preschool registration" signs (with arrows pointing to the Preschool Bible SpacePlace) near your main registration area.

On the preschool registration table(s), place

- a copy of each completed preschool "Age-Level Roster" (p. 145),
- a copy of each preschool "Flight Crew Roster" (p. 146),
- blank copies of the "Registration Form" (p. 148), and
- several pencils.

Registration:
Here They Come!

1. Arrange for your registration workers (including Flight Crew Leaders) to arrive at least thirty minutes *before* registration is scheduled to begin.

2. Cut apart the individual "Flight Crew Roster" lists from the third set of "Flight Crew Roster" lists you copied. As Flight Crew Leaders arrive, give each a copy of his or her crew roster.

3. Send elementary Flight Crew Leaders to the Sing & Play Blast Off area and preschool Flight Crew Leaders to Preschool Bible SpacePlace. Explain that as kids arrive, they'll find their Flight Crew numbers at the registration tables and then join their crew leaders and other Flight Crew members in Sing & Play Blast Off or Preschool Bible SpacePlace.

4. Assign two workers to the preregistration table, two workers to the walk-in table, and at least one worker to the preschool table.

5. Go over the registration instructions for each area (preregistered, walk-in registration, and preschool). Answer any questions workers have, and offer the following helpful hints:

- Kindly insist that each participant fill out a complete registration form, including all pertinent health and emergency information. *This is very important!*
- If families have both preschool and elementary children, encourage them to go to the preschool area first. This will keep preschoolers from getting fidgety as they wait for their parents to register their older siblings.
- Walk-in registration will naturally take more time. As families are filling out their registration forms, scan the Flight Crew rosters for openings. This will help you complete Flight Crew assignments quickly.

After you've answered all the questions, have registration workers and Flight Crew Leaders take their places. You're ready to welcome kids to Space Mission Bible Camp!

Important!

It's important that you know at all times who is in each Flight Crew. In an emergency or if a parent needs to pick up a child midprogram, you'll want an accurate "map" of where everyone is.

Registration

141

After Registration

After registration on Day 1, shout out a loud, "Blast off!" Your biggest job is done! Read on to find out how you can ensure that Days 2 through 5 are successful.

● **Leave your registration tables in place.** You'll want to continue welcoming children as they arrive on Days 2 through 5, as well as registering any newcomers. Tape the "Alphabetical Master List" to the table, and set out several pencils or pens. To chart attendance, let children (or parents) check each day's box as they come to Space Mission Bible Camp.

● **Check in with Training Station Leaders and Flight Crew Leaders.** Even if you've mapped everything out ahead of time, unforeseen glitches can make your mission miserable! After you've gone through one day's activities, meet with your space-camp staff to evaluate how things went. Training Station Leaders may find that they need additional supplies or alternative room assignments. Inexperienced Flight Crew Leaders may be having trouble handling unruly children in their Flight Crews. If this is the case, you may need to reassign some children to different crews or rearrange your groups so that Flight Crews with inexperienced leaders visit Training Stations with crews that have experienced leaders.

● **Update your "Alphabetical Master List" and "Flight Crew Rosters" as needed.** Be sure to check with the volunteers at the walk-in table. Kids who completed walk-in registration on Day 1 can be added to the "Alphabetical Master List" for speedier check-in through the rest of the week. If you've rearranged your Flight Crews, make sure each Flight Crew receives an updated "Flight Crew Roster."

Mission accomplished! Now sit back and soar through your week!

Space Mission Bible Camp
Registration Instructions

Photocopy these instructions, and place copies in all registration areas. Have registration workers highlight their areas of responsibility.

Preschool: Preregistered and Walk-In

Preschool registration will take place _____.

1. Greet family members or caregivers with a warm smile. Thank them for bringing the children to Space Mission Bible Camp.
2. Ask for each child's name and age (three, four, or five years old). Greet each child by name, and thank him or her for coming.

If a child has completed kindergarten or is older than six, send the family to the elementary preregistered line.

3. Have parents or caregivers complete registration forms for unregistered children.
4. Locate each registered child's name on the "Alphabetical Master List," and place a check mark on the Day 1 box to indicate that he or she is present.
5. If a child is a walk-in, scan the preschool "Flight Crew Roster" lists to find an appropriate Flight Crew to place him or her in. Add the child's name to the "Flight Crew Roster" list as well as to the "Alphabetical Master List."
6. Point out the child's Flight Crew Leader, and have a Preschool Bible SpacePlace volunteer guide the child to the Flight Crew Leader.
7. Tell the family members or caregivers that they can pick up their preschoolers in the Mission Send-Off Show Time area each day. Assure them that an adult or teenage Flight Crew Leader will stay with children until the family members or caregivers arrive.

Registration

Elementary: Preregistered

Elementary registration will take place _____.

1. Greet family members or caregivers with a warm smile. Thank them for bringing the children to Space Mission Bible Camp.
2. Ask for each child's name and the grade he or she last completed (kindergarten through fifth grade). Greet each child by name, and thank him or her for coming.

If a child has not yet attended kindergarten, send the family to Preschool Bible SpacePlace for registration.

3. Locate each child's name on the "Alphabetical Master List" or, if a child's name isn't on the list, send the family to the walk-in table to complete a new registration form.
4. Put a check mark by each child's name to indicate that he or she is present at Space Mission Bible Camp. Then tell the child his or her Flight Crew number and crew leader's name.
5. Direct children to the Sing & Play Blast Off area, and explain that crew leaders are waiting there with name badges. Tell children to look for a large sign with their crew number on it.
6. Tell the family members or caregivers what time they can pick up their children each day. Encourage them to come early and participate in Mission Send-Off Show Time.

Space Mission Bible Camp
Registration Instructions

Elementary: Walk-In Registration

Elementary registration will take place at _____.

1. Greet family members or caregivers with a warm smile. Thank them for bringing the children to Space Mission Bible Camp.
2. Ask for each child's name and the grade he or she last completed (kindergarten through fifth grade). Greet each child by name, and thank him or her for coming.

If a child has not yet attended kindergarten, send the family to Preschool Bible SpacePlace for registration.

3. Add each child's name to the appropriate "Age-Level Roster." Have the child's parent or caregiver complete a registration form.
4. While parents fill out registration forms, assign each child to a Flight Crew. Refer to the "Flight Crew Rosters" to see which crews have openings. Look for a Flight Crew *without* a member in that child's grade. *If you have questions about assigning children to Flight Crews, see your Mission Control Director!*
5. Write each child's Flight Crew number on his or her completed registration form. (Later you'll need to add the new name and Flight Crew assignment to the "Alphabetical Master List.")
6. Direct children to the Sing & Play Blast Off area, and explain that crew leaders are waiting there with name badges. Tell children to look for a sign with their crew number on it.
7. Tell the family members or caregivers what time they can pick up their children each day. Encourage them to come early and participate in Mission Send-Off Show Time.

Age-Level Roster

Grade: _____

_____   _____

_____   _____

_____   _____

_____   _____

_____   _____

_____   _____

_____   _____

_____   _____

_____   _____

_____   _____

_____   _____

_____   _____

_____   _____

_____   _____

Registration

Flight Crew Roster

Crew Number: _____

Flight Crew Leader: _____

Crew Members:

1. _____
2. _____
3. _____
4. _____
5. _____

Crew Number: _____

Flight Crew Leader: _____

Crew Members:

1. _____
2. _____
3. _____
4. _____
5. _____

Crew Number: _____

Flight Crew Leader: _____

Crew Members:

1. _____
2. _____
3. _____
4. _____
5. _____

Crew Number: _____

Flight Crew Leader: _____

Crew Members:

1. _____
2. _____
3. _____
4. _____
5. _____

Alphabetical Master List

Name	Flight Crew Number	Day 1	Day 2	Day 3	Day 4	Day 5
_____	_____	☐	☐	☐	☐	☐
_____	_____	☐	☐	☐	☐	☐
_____	_____	☐	☐	☐	☐	☐
_____	_____	☐	☐	☐	☐	☐
_____	_____	☐	☐	☐	☐	☐
_____	_____	☐	☐	☐	☐	☐
_____	_____	☐	☐	☐	☐	☐
_____	_____	☐	☐	☐	☐	☐
_____	_____	☐	☐	☐	☐	☐
_____	_____	☐	☐	☐	☐	☐
_____	_____	☐	☐	☐	☐	☐
_____	_____	☐	☐	☐	☐	☐
_____	_____	☐	☐	☐	☐	☐
_____	_____	☐	☐	☐	☐	☐
_____	_____	☐	☐	☐	☐	☐
_____	_____	☐	☐	☐	☐	☐
_____	_____	☐	☐	☐	☐	☐
_____	_____	☐	☐	☐	☐	☐
_____	_____	☐	☐	☐	☐	☐
_____	_____	☐	☐	☐	☐	☐

Registration

Space Mission Bible Camp
Registration Form

Name: _____

Street address: _____

City: _____ State: _____ ZIP: _____

Home Telephone: (___) _____ Age: _____

Last school grade completed: _____

In case of emergency, contact: _____

Mother: _____

Father: _____

Other: _____

Allergies or other medical conditions: _____

Home church: _____

Flight Crew number (for church use only): _____

Spaceship Tips

Secrets for a Successful Space Mission

Bells and Whistles

You have all the basic Space Mission Bible Camp materials in your Starter Kit. If you want to add sparkle and pizazz to your program, check out some of the following items.

Training Station Leader Resources

● **Space whistle**—You and your Training Station Leaders will keep kids' attention the easy way with bright, colorful space whistles. Children love the cheerful "wheeee" sound and will easily hear it in a crowded room or on a playing field. As Mission Control Director, you'll use a space whistle to let Flight Crews know when it's time to "blast off" to their next Training Stations. Encourage Training Station Leaders to use the whistles any time they need to get kids' attention.

● *Sing & Play Blast Off* **audiocassette or** *Sing & Play Blast Off Music & Clip Art CD*—Reinforce Bible learning by providing each Training Station Leader with his or her own *Sing & Play Blast Off* audiocassette or CD. Kids can hum along as they create Space Crafts, play Have-a-Blast Games, and enjoy Mission Munchies. You can also offer this audiocassette or CD to families to reinforce Bible learning at home.

● *Sing & Play Blast Off Song Lyrics Transparencies*—Project song lyrics onto a large screen to make it even easier for kids (and adults) to follow along.

● **Mission Munchies chef hat**—Tall, starched, and white, this classic paper chef hat helps your Mission Munchies Leader look the part! Order one for your Mission Munchies Leader, or order several so kids can join in the food-preparation fun.

● *Preschool Bible SpacePlace* **audiocassette**—Provide upbeat music for your youngest astronauts. This cassette includes the Space Mission Bible Camp theme song, "Little Bit of Love," as well as other special songs and stories just for preschoolers.

Additional Space Mission Resources

● **Space Mission Bible Camp iron-on transfers**—These colorful transfers allow adults and children to create wearable mementos of their space mission.

● **Space Mission Bible Camp photo frames**—Help kids remember Space Mission Bible Camp fun. These sturdy four-by-six-inch cardboard frames feature the Space Mission Bible Camp logo and provide plenty of room for you to add your church's name and address. Insert inexpensive photos you've shot during your program, and offer them for sale—or give them to children as special gifts they'll treasure all summer!

● **Space Mission Bible Camp photo backdrop poster**—Create extra-special photos with this full-color, oversize Space Mission Bible Camp backdrop. Hang the backdrop on a wall or have volunteers hold it up. Kids can step right up as your photographer snaps their pictures.

● **Chadder Chipmunk items**—Chadder is now available in three sizes: small hand puppet, larger plush puppet, and adult-size costume pattern (for any adult "chipmunk-wannabe!"). Preschoolers will love having Chadder visit their room. The Preschool Bible SpacePlace Director Manual suggests ways to make this furry friend part of your Space Mission Bible Camp program. You can give Chadder puppets to volunteers to thank them for their help or you can use Chadder puppets to reinforce Bible learning at other children's ministry events.

Pilot Program Pointer

"My child hasn't stopped singing those Space Mission Bible Camp songs!" We hear this so often, and—we admit— we smile every time! It's great to know that kids are singing phrases such as "I believe in Jesus..." or "J-E-S-U-S, yes! He's my everything!" That's why we believe it's so important to get these resources into homes everywhere.

Taking Home Space Mission Fun

Why Are Family Resources So Important?

Your Space Mission Bible Camp will reach a variety of children from countless backgrounds. Each of these children (and their families) can benefit from having Space Mission Bible Camp resources at home. Not only do the following family resources remind kids of Space Mission Bible Camp fun, but they also provide excellent Bible reinforcement for months after your program has ended. A *Sing & Play Blast Off* audiocassette may be the only Christian music heard in some children's homes.

What Are Family Resources?

In the front of each Student Book, you'll find an order form that lists seven family resources that reinforce Bible learning. (You'll also find the same form on page 154 of this manual if you want to photocopy the form and send it home.) From our pilot programs, we know that kids love items such as the *Sing & Play Blast Off* audiocassette and CD, the *Sing & Play Blast Off Music Video,* and *Chadder's Space Mission Adventure* videotapes. In fact, several parents arrived early on Day 5 so they could be sure to purchase the limited number of cassettes we had!

Kids love to have mementos of their time at Space Mission Bible Camp. Items such as Chadder plush puppets and iron-on transfers are great reminders of your program.

How Can Families Get These Resources?

We realize you're busy; after all, you've just coordinated a VBS program! So we've made it simple to get these important items into the hands of the kids in your program. In the front of each Student Book, you'll find an order form for seven family resources. Now you have two options:

Option 1: Individual Orders

Point out the Student Book order form at the end of Sing & Play Blast Off on Day 5. Let kids know that they can order the Sing & Play Blast Off music, Chadder videos, and other fun stuff simply by taking the order form to their local Christian bookstore. Then send the Student Books home, and let kids and their families act from there.

Option 2: One Church Order

Point out the Student Book order form at the end of Sing & Play Blast Off on Day 5. Let kids know that they can order the Sing & Play Blast Off music, Chadder videos, and other fun stuff by having a parent help them fill out the order form. Tell kids they'll then need to bring their money and order form (in an envelope) to you by a specified date. You'll probably want to put the date in your church bulletin the following Sunday.

After the due date, tally the total number of each item, and fill it in on a blank order form or a photocopy of the form on page 154 of this manual. Be sure to keep the original order forms so you can distribute items accurately! Take the master order form to your local Christian bookstore, and purchase the items. The next Sunday, set up a table to distribute Space Mission Bible Camp materials.

It's that easy!

STUDENT ORDER FORM

Name _____

Address _____

_____

City _____ State _____ Zip _____

Phone _____

Complete this order form and return it to your VBS director. Or inquire at your local Christian bookstore for these great *Space Mission Bible Camp* items!

HOW MANY	TITLE	ITEM NO.	PRICE	TOTAL COST
	1. *Sing & Play Blast Off* Audiocassette	#98054	$10.99	
	2. *Sing & Play Blast Off* Music & Clip Art CD	#98062	$12.99	
	3. *Sing & Play Blast Off* Music Video	#98013	$19.99	
	4. *Chadder's Space Mission Adventure!* Video	#98003	$19.99	
	5. Iron-On Transfers (Pkg. of 10)	#9043	$11.99	
	6. Home Mission Activity Panel	#98231	$3.99	
	7. Chadder Plush Puppet	#9056	$35.99	

Subtotal $_____

Shipping & Handling $_____

Sales tax (CA 7.25%, CO 3%, GA 4%, IA 5%, OH 5%) $_____

TOTAL $_____

You can also mail this completed order form and payment to:
Group Publishing, Inc., P.O. Box 485, Loveland, CO 80539

PLEASE ADD SHIPPING & HANDLING FROM THE CHART BELOW.

SHIPPING & HANDLING	ORDER SUBTOTAL	SHIPPING & HANDLING
	Up to $12	$3.50
	$12.01-$20.00	$4.90
	$20.01-$50.00	$5.90
	$50.01-$75.00	$7.90
	$75.01-$100.00	$11.90
	$100.01-$150.00	$15.90
	$150.01-$200.00	$19.90
	$200.01+	$24.90

Spaceship Tips

Health and Safety Concerns

Each Training Station leader manual gives safety tips for specific Training Station activities. As Mission Control Director, however, you're responsible for larger health and safety concerns that may affect the entire camp. The information below may alert you to health and safety concerns that require your attention.

Health Issues

You'll want to maintain a first-aid kit in a central location. Stock your first-aid kit with adhesive bandages of different sizes, first-aid cream, antibacterial ointment, sterile gauze pads, and insect repellent. You may also want to provide a place for children to lie down if they feel ill. Keep children's registration forms near your first-aid area so you can call parents or caregivers in case of serious injury.

Your Space Mission Bible Camp registration form provides a spot for parents or caregivers to identify food allergies. Dairy allergies are common, but you may also have children who are allergic to gluten (wheat, rye, barley, or oats); nuts; or other foods.

Most of the snacks suggested in the Mission Munchies Leader Manual will require only slight modifications for children with food allergies. Consult with the Mission Munchies Leader about modifying snacks or about substituting flavored rice cakes, popcorn, fruits, or raw vegetables to accommodate children with food allergies.

Insurance: Make Sure You're Covered

Your church probably already has an insurance policy or policies that are intended to protect you from loss as a result of fire, theft, injury, or lawsuits. Your program is probably covered by your regular insurance, but you should double-check with your insurance agent to be sure. You're not likely to have serious injuries, but you'll want to be prepared just in case.

Facilities: Maintaining a Spick-and-Span Space Station

Many accidents can be prevented by well-maintained facilities. After you've selected Training Station meeting areas, check each area for potential hazards. Remove broken or dangerous items, and be sure to lock storage areas that contain chemicals, cleaning solutions, or other toxic materials.

Your church is about to become a high-traffic area! Keep in mind that you'll probably need to clean bathrooms and empty trash daily. You'll also want to spot-check hallways, lobbies, and meeting rooms for trash, stray crew tote bags, and lost-and-found items.

Child Abuse: Keeping Kids Safe

Child abuse can take many forms. While you may feel sure that no one in your church would physically or sexually abuse a child in your program, emotional abuse or neglect can be harder to detect. Prevent child abuse by enlisting only staff members that you know and trust and by discussing your concerns and expectations with them ahead of time.

Space Mission Bible Camp pilot program directors reported few or no discipline problems. But you'll want to talk with your staff about how you'll handle any that do arise. Discuss appropriate and inappropriate staff responses to situations that require discipline. Photocopy and distribute the "What's a Flight Crew Leader?" handout from page 111 of this manual. This handout suggests positive-language responses for easy classroom management. Remind staff members that you expect them to model God's love in all they say and do.

Space Mission Bible Camp activities are designed so that children are always supervised by a Training Station Leader and several Flight Crew Leaders. You may want to point this out to parents who are concerned about adequate supervision. To avoid even the appearance of impropriety, encourage each staff member to avoid spending time alone with a child. Suggest that staff members escort children in pairs or small groups for bathroom and drinking fountain stops.

Use these health and safety tips to set up a Space Mission Bible Camp program that ensures the physical, emotional, and spiritual well-being of everyone involved.

Kids With Special Needs

Physical Disabilities

If you know you'll have physically challenged children at your program, you'll need to make sure your Training Station areas are wheelchair accessible. You may also want to recruit a staff member to look out for these children. This staff member can ask parents or caretakers about specific needs such as

- whether kids have special equipment such as wheelchairs,
- what kids can and cannot eat,
- what kids need help doing,
- what kids like to do for themselves, and
- what kids enjoy most.

Because children work together and help each other in Flight Crews, most physically challenged children will get the help they need from their crew members and Flight Crew Leaders. However, if a physically challenged child needs constant help to participate in Training Station activities, consider assigning an additional Flight Crew Leader to his or her crew. For this position, choose someone who will be sensitive and who is capable of responding to the child's needs.

Physically challenged children may be shy, but often they're very bright and innovative. Flight Crew Leaders can encourage them to shine in Training Stations that include group discussion, such as Chadder's Space Mission Theater or Bible Exploration. (Plus, as kids carry out their crew roles, they'll all discover how important each crew member is!)

Learning Disabilities

Educators estimate that up to 20 percent of today's children have some type of learning disability. That means that in a program of one hundred children, up to twenty kids could be battling with dyslexia, attention-deficit/hyperactivity disorder, or other learning disabilities. Kids with learning disabilities aren't lazy or dumb—they just learn differently than other children do.

Space Mission Bible Camp works for children with learning disabilities! Here's why:

- **It doesn't rely on reading skills.** Children who enjoy reading can volunteer to be Readers for their Flight Crews. Children who have trouble reading can choose other equally important jobs.
- **It allows kids processing time.** Because each Flight Crew has a Flight

Pilot Program Pointer

Everyone *can do the activities at Space Mission Bible Camp! A physically challenged boy attended our pilot program, and he jumped right in and tried it all. Some activities were more challenging, but with the help of his crew members and a little flexibility, he was able to fully participate in every activity. What a wonderful reminder that God can use all of us to carry out his mission of love!*

Crew Leader, Training Station Leaders don't have to single out kids who need special help. Crew leaders can help the kids in their Flight Crews work at their own pace. And Training Station Leaders are free to go around and check in with children as they complete their activities.

● **It doesn't require children to think sequentially.** Fifty percent of all students are frustrated by sequential-type assignments. At Space Mission Bible Camp, children don't have to master a new set of information each day. Instead, they learn one basic Point that's reinforced in different ways for different kinds of learners.

If you know or suspect that kids with learning disabilities will be attending your program, let your teachers know. Encourage them to help these children by

● giving instructions one at a time,
● using the positive-language suggestions in the "What's a Flight Crew Leader?" handout (p. 111),
● ignoring harmless annoying behaviors, and
● praising children sincerely and often.

For more information on attention-deficit/hyperactivity disorder (ADHD), use the address below to contact Children and Adults with Attention Deficit Disorders.

Children and Adults with Attention Deficit Disorders
499 N.W. 70th Ave. #101
Plantation, Florida 33317
(954) 587-3700

Welcoming Newcomers

Summer is a busy time for families. Some kids may come to Space Mission Bible Camp all five days; some may come for two or three days and then drop out; others may join your Space Mission Bible Camp program midcourse. Use the following ideas to welcome newcomers to your camp.

● **Start with small Flight Crews.** When you assign kids to Flight Crews, limit some crews to three or four kids instead of five. If new kids join your program, you can assign them to Flight Crews in which you've left openings. Even if you don't have many visitors, kids in smaller crews will love the additional attention they'll get from their Flight Crew Leaders. If you want to encourage visitors to attend, challenge kids to fill their crews by inviting their friends!

● **Have kids introduce new Flight Crew members.** Instead of escorting a visitor to a Flight Crew yourself, invite one of the crew members to do it. Recruit an outgoing member of the visitor's assigned crew (a Cheerleader may be a good candidate for this job), and then introduce the visitor to the other child one on one. Help the child describe the Flight Crew, including the crew name, the crew jobs, and the daily schedule. Then send the pair of children back to meet the rest of the crew.

● **Cheer for visitors each day during Sing & Play Blast Off.** Have the Sing & Play Blast Off Leader invite Flight Crews to stand if they have new members. Have Cheerleaders introduce their new crew members; then have the Sing & Play Blast Off Leader lead everyone in a countdown from ten to zero, followed by shouting, "Welcome!"

Responsibility: Let 'Em Have It!

At Space Mission Bible Camp, Training Station Leaders provide fun, hands-on, Bible-learning activities. Flight Crew Leaders shepherd and guide their Flight Crews. But kids take responsibility for their own learning.

Even the most well-intentioned Training Station Leaders and Flight Crew Leaders may be uncomfortable giving kids this much responsibility. After all, they're the leaders—they've prepared the material, and they know what kids should learn. Mission Munchies Leaders may insist that it's easier to prepare snacks ahead of time instead of counting on kids to complete the work. Flight Crew Leaders may be tempted to complete Space Crafts for kids instead of helping them complete their own.

Every activity at your Space Mission Bible Camp program has been field-tested, revised, retested, and revised again. So you can have confidence that kids will be able to follow directions and complete the activities successfully within the allotted times. Instead of doing kids' work for them, leaders should encourage Flight Crew members to carry out their mission of God's love by helping each other complete activities.

By the end of the week, you'll hear reports of kids leading their own discussions, helping each other complete projects, and cheering each other on. Trust the Lord, and trust your kids—and watch God's love surround your program!

Returning to Earth

Closing Program and Follow-Up Ideas

Helping Children Follow Jesus

At Space Mission Bible Camp, children don't just hear about God's love—they see it, touch it, sing it, taste it, and put it into action. As they travel from Training Station to Training Station, they discover that God helps us be kind, thankful, helpful, and faithful. Most importantly, children learn that God sent his Son, Jesus, to die for our sins because he loves us.

You'll notice that there's no "set" time for children to make a faith commitment. We feel that Space Mission Bible Camp helps children build relationships—with other children, adults, and with Jesus. And since each child is at a different point in his or her relationship with Jesus, programming a time for commitment may be confusing to some children. However, if it's part of your church tradition to include a time for children to make a faith decision, feel free to add it in during the Mission Send-Off Show Time on Day 4.

Some children may want to know more about making Jesus part of their lives. If you sense that a child might like to know more about what it means to follow Jesus, give this simple explanation:

God loves us so much that he sent his Son, Jesus, to die on the cross for us. Jesus died and rose again so we could be forgiven for all the wrong things we do. Jesus wants to be our forever friend. If we ask him to, he'll take away the wrong things we've done and fill our hearts with his love. As our forever friend, Jesus will always be with us and will help us make the right choices. And if we believe in Jesus, someday we'll live with him forever in heaven.

You may want to lead the child in a simple prayer inviting Jesus to be his or her forever friend. You may also want to share one or more of the following Scripture passages with the child. Encourage the child to read the Scripture passages with you from his or her own Bible.

- John 3:16
- Romans 5:8-11
- Romans 6:23
- Ephesians 2:5-8

Be sure to share the news of the child's spiritual development with his or her parent(s).

Mission Accomplished!

Thanks for joining us at Group's Space Mission Bible Camp! Now that you've completed your mission, you can sit back, relax, and congratulate yourself and your staff on a job well done. Then thank God for his blessings on your program. In this section, you'll find ideas that will help you to wrap up your program and follow up with children and their families. You'll also find helpful evaluation forms you can use to get specific feedback from Training Station Leaders and Flight Crew Leaders.

Closing Program: Coming Back to Earth

If you want an easy way to give parents and church members a glimpse of your Space Mission Bible Camp fun, invite them to attend Mission Send-Off Show Time. This fun-filled, Bible-learning time is already built in to your Space Mission Bible Camp program each day. Explain that parents can join the fun by arriving just twenty minutes early when they come to pick up their children. They'll see children singing Sing & Play Blast Off songs, telling about their daily missions, and actively reviewing the daily Bible story. Parents will really catch the Space Mission Bible Camp spirit as children celebrate God's love with colorful signs, costumes, and cheers on Day 5.

If you want to have a separate closing program, follow the steps below to set up a Training Station "open house." Set up your open house in the evening or even on Sunday morning. Parents and kids will love it!

1. Have Training Station Leaders set up the following activities in their respective Training Station areas. If you purchased additional *Sing & Play Blast Off* audiocassettes, encourage Training Station Leaders to play the Space Mission Bible Camp songs while people are visiting their areas.

Sing & Play Blast Off—Have the Sing & Play Blast Off Leader teach words and motions to all thirteen songs (or as many as time allows).

Preschool Bible SpacePlace—Have the Preschool Bible SpacePlace Director set up five or six Blast Off Discovery Stations children can visit with their parents. Choose from the activities suggested below or let the Preschool Bible SpacePlace Director suggest kids' favorites!

- Craters and Pits (Day 1)
- Squishy Fishies (Day 3)
- Follow-Me Comets (Day 4)

Space Crafts—Have the Space Crafts Leader display his or her sample Space Crafts (or have kids display the crafts they made—if they're willing to part with them for a little while). Ask the crafts leader to explain the stories of Danse, Pilar, and Yang Ky on the "Operation Kid-to-Kid" posters. Have the crafts leader encourage kids to show their parents how to launch their Blast Off Rockets.

Have-a-Blast Games—Have the games leader lead families in the Impossible Loop Pass kids played on Day 3 or Space Spinners from Day 4. Families will also enjoy playing Kindness Cliques (Day 1) or Hannah's Hot Seat (Day 2).

Mission Munchies—Have the Mission Munchies Leader set out supplies for making Jail Cell Snackers (Day 5). Display a sample snack, and let children and parents make their own tasty treats.

Chadder's Space Mission Theater—Have the Chadder's Space Mission Theater Leader play the *Chadder's Space Mission Adventure* video. Set out paper, markers, and pencils, and let families write letters of advice to Chadder or draw pictures of him.

Bible Exploration—Have the Bible Exploration Leader set up the pit (Day 1) and take groups inside the pit to hear the story of Joseph. Parents can hold the flashlights under their chins to make the angry faces of Joseph's brothers. You may want to provide tiny flashlight key chains for each family to remind them that when we're kind, we're like a light that leads others to God.

Mission Send-Off Show Time—Have the Mission Send-Off Show Time Leader lead people in the show from Day 4. Let parents squirt the disappearing ink on Jesus' robe. Have families join together to sing "We Must Believe" and talk about ways they can show others that they believe in Jesus.

2. Begin by having everyone gather in the sanctuary or the fellowship hall for a brief introduction and a Sing & Play Blast Off time. Have your Sing & Play Blast Off Leader teach everyone "Little Bit of Love." This is a great time to distribute Space Mission Bible Camp completion certificates. Simply photocopy the certificates on pages 168 and 169 (or purchase the "Mission Accomplished!" certificates); fill in children's, Flight Crew Leaders', or Training Station Leaders' names; then sign and date each certificate.

3. Designate a thirty- to forty-five-minute time frame in which families can visit the Training Stations. At the end of the designated time, use a space whistle to call everyone back to your original meeting area for Mission

Send-Off Show Time.

4. Thank everyone for coming, and encourage them to join you in planning and preparing for next year's program.

Follow-Up Ideas

Your Space Mission Bible Camp has landed. But your mission of God's love isn't over yet—you still have lots of time to share the good news about Jesus with the kids in your church and community. The outreach efforts you make will help you share God's love with your Space Mission Bible Camp participants and their families. Use the ideas below to design a follow-up plan that fits your church's needs.

● **Send Space Mission Bible Camp follow-up postcards.** Kids love getting mail, so here's a sure-fire way to get kids back for Sunday school—a personal invitation from Space Mission Bible Camp. These colorful postcards help you make a long-term impact on kids by involving them in your regular Sunday school program. *Order these postcards from Group Publishing and your local Christian bookstore.*

● **Give away Space Mission Bible Camp photos.** Deliver framed photos to families of children who don't regularly attend your church. Kids will treasure these colorful, fun mementos—and you'll have an opportunity to invite the family to visit your church. *Order Space Mission Bible Camp photo frames from Group Publishing and your local Christian bookstore.*

● **Invite Chadder Chipmunk to visit a children's ministry event.** Schedule a return engagement of *Chadder's Space Mission Adventure* during another children's ministry event. Children who visited your church during Space Mission Bible Camp will want to come back and revisit their furry friend. Add a live appearance from a Chadder plush puppet, and you'll be sure to fill every chair! *Order Chadder plush puppets, costume patterns, and* Chadder's Space Mission Adventure *videocassettes from Group Publishing and your local Christian bookstore.*

● **Give out "blast-off buddies" adoption certificates.** Use Space Mission Bible Camp registration forms to make certificates, each containing a child's vital statistics: birthday, age, likes, interests, address, phone number, and family information. (This is a great job for Flight Crew Leaders—they've probably collected a wealth of information about the kids in their Flight Crews!) Then connect each child with a church family. Families can use the certificates to get to know their "adoptees" throughout the year, pray for their adoptees, and encourage them to attend church and Sunday school.

● **Sponsor a parents day.** Build relationships with children's parents by having a parents day during Space Mission Bible Camp. Encourage children to invite their parents or older siblings to join them. Provide adult and youth Bible studies or have family members visit the Training Stations with their children's Flight Crews. Also, require parents to come inside to pick up their children so you can make contact with them.

● **Hold a Space Mission memory night.** Invite all the Space Mission Bible Camp participants to a get-together every month or every quarter. Make each memory night a fun event that fits the Space Mission Bible Camp Theme. For example, set out aluminum foil, empty milk cartons, stickers, and craft sticks, and encourage kids to create wild space crafts. You'll want to include yummy Mission Munchies at each memory night!

Mission Accomplished!

Thanks for
Launching Kids on a Mission of God's Love

at SPACE MISSION Bible Camp™

You've been an out-of-this-world

_____
Mission Control Director

_____
Date

Mission Accomplished!

Thanks, _____, for training at

SPACE MISSION Bible Camp™

We had a blast on our mission of God's love!

_____
Mission Control Director

_____
Date

Follow-Up Ideas

Thank These "Stars" Who Made

SPACE MISSION *Bible Camp*™

Such a Blast!

Follow-Up Ideas

Evaluating Your Space Mission Bible Camp Program

After Space Mission Bible Camp, you'll want to check in with your Training Station Leaders, Flight Crew Leaders, and other staff members to see how things went.

Photocopy the "Training Station Leader VBS Evaluation" (p. 172) and the "Flight Crew Leader VBS Evaluation" (p. 173), and distribute the photocopies to your staff. To help your evaluation process go smoothly, you may want to ask staff members to return their evaluations within two weeks of Space Mission Bible Camp. After two weeks, specific details will still be fresh in staff members' minds, and they'll have a good perspective on their overall experiences.

After you've collected Training Station Leader and Flight Crew Leader evaluation forms, please take a few moments to fill out the "Space Mission Bible Camp Evaluation" on pages 175-176. Be sure to summarize the comments you received from Training Station Leaders and Flight Crew Leaders. Keep a copy of your completed evaluation for your records; then return the original to Group's VBS Coordinator. Your detailed feedback will help us meet your needs as we plan an all-new program for next year.

Thanks for Choosing Group's Space Mission Bible Camp!

Spaceship Tip

You can customize the evaluation forms by adding additional questions in the "other comments about our Space Mission Bible Camp program" section. For example, you may want to ask about facilities or about the dates and times of your VBS. This is also a good time to recruit volunteers for next year's VBS. Training Station Leaders and Flight Crew Leaders will have had so much fun that they'll want to sign on again!

Training Station Leader
VBS Evaluation

Thanks for joining us at Space Mission Bible Camp! Please complete this evaluation form to help us plan for next year's VBS.

1. I led the _____ Training Station.

2. I spent _____ minutes preparing materials for each day.

3. Were the instructions in your Training Station leader manual clear and easy to follow? Explain.

4. What did you like best about your Training Station? What did kids like best?

5. What would you like to change about your Training Station?

Other comments about our Space Mission Bible Camp program:

Follow-Up Ideas

Flight Crew Leader VBS Evaluation

Thanks for joining us at Space Mission Bible Camp! Please complete this evaluation form to help us plan for next year's VBS.

1. What was the best thing about working with your Flight Crew?

2. What was the hardest thing?

3. Did the "For Flight Crew Leaders Only" handouts help you as you worked with kids? Explain.

4. What other training helps or resources would have helped you in your Flight Crew Leader role?

Follow-Up Ideas

■ ■ ■ Space Mission Bible Camp Evaluation ■ ■ ■

Thanks for blasting off with us!

We appreciate your joining us for unforgettable, fun Bible learning...and we look forward to introducing you to an all-new VBS next year!

Will you help us make next year's VBS even better? Take a few moments at the end of your program to fill out this survey. Drop it in the mail, and let us know what you think!

Thank you!

Jody Brolsma

Jody Brolsma
Space Mission Bible Camp Coordinator

- -
FOLD   FOLD

1. What was the number one reason you chose Group's Space Mission Bible Camp?

2. Tell us how you learned about Group's Space Mission Bible Camp.
- ○ Bookstore
- ○ Mailing
- ○ Advertisement
- ○ Other (please specify)

3. Where did you purchase your VBS items?
- ○ Bookstore
- ○ Direct from Group

4. Tell us how you liked the Space Mission Bible Camp program.
- ○ I loved it! I can't wait to see next year's!
- ○ It was OK—it met my VBS needs.
- ○ It didn't work at all for my church.

What, if anything, would you like us to change or improve?

Would you consider using a Group VBS program next summer?
- ○ Absolutely—here's why...
- ○ Maybe—here's why...
- ○ No way—here's why...

Comments:

- -
FOLD   FOLD

5. Tell us what was most difficult for you in putting together Space Mission Bible Camp.

What could we do to make your job easier?

6. Tell us what you liked most about the Mission Control Director Manual.

What would you change about the Mission Control Director Manual?

7. Tell us about your church's VBS program.
- Dates: _____
- Times: _____
- Number of participants: _____
- Summarize comments from VBS participants and families:

8. Tell us about the music at your VBS.

If you used the *Sing & Play Music Video,* how did it help your program?

Did you use the clip art on the CD?

9. Tell us about your Training Stations.

Were your Training Stations easy to set up and lead?

What could we do to make it easier for Training Station Leaders to do their jobs?

Summarize comments from your Training Station Leaders:

FOLD   FOLD

10. How did kids respond to the *Chadder's Space Mission Adventure* video?

11. Tell us about Operation Kid-to-Kid.

What did you like about the mission project?

Would you like to see a mission incorporated each year?

12. We're always looking for fun and innovative themes for our VBS programs. What new ideas would you like to see in the future?

13. If you've seen a life changed as a result of your VBS, please share the story.

If you said something nice about Group's VBS, may we quote you?   ◯ yes

Please fold on dotted lines with the below flap facing outside and tape closed. Thank you.

NAME _____

ADDRESS_____

CITY _____ STATE _____ ZIP _____

||| ||

NO POSTAGE
NECESSARY
IF MAILED
IN THE
UNITED STATES

BUSINESS REPLY MAIL
FIRST-CLASS MAIL   PERMIT NO 16   LOVELAND CO

POSTAGE WILL BE PAID BY ADDRESSEE

VBS COORDINATOR
P.O. BOX 481
LOVELAND, CO 80539-9985

|||||||||||||||||||||||||||||||||||||||||||||||||

Index

TEACH YOUR PRESCHOOLERS AS JESUS TAUGHT WITH GROUP'S *HANDS-ON BIBLE CURRICULUM*™

Hands-On Bible Curriculum™ **for preschoolers** helps your preschoolers learn the way they learn best—by touching, exploring, and discovering. With active learning, preschoolers love learning about the Bible, and they really remember what they learn.

Because small children learn best through repetition, Preschoolers and Pre-K & K will learn one important point per lesson, and Toddlers & 2s will learn one point each month with **Hands-On Bible Curriculum**. These important lessons will stick with them and comfort them during their daily lives. Your children will learn God is our friend, who Jesus is, and we can always trust Jesus.

The **Learning Lab**® is packed with age-appropriate learning tools for fun, faith-building lessons. Toddlers & 2s explore big **Interactive StoryBoards**™ with enticing textures that toddlers love to touch—like sandpaper for earth, cotton for clouds, and blue cellophane for water. While they hear the Bible story, children also *touch* the Bible story. And they learn. **Bible Big Books**™ captivate Preschoolers and Pre-K & K while teaching them important Bible lessons. With **Jumbo Bible Puzzles**™ and involving **Learning Mats**™, your children will see, touch, and explore their Bible stories. Each quarter there's a brand new collection of supplies to keep your lessons fresh and involving.

Just order one **Learning Lab** and one **Teacher Guide** for each age level, add a few common classroom supplies, and presto—you have everything you need to inspire and build faith in your children. For more interactive fun, introduce your children to the age-appropriate puppet (Cuddles the Lamb, Whiskers the Mouse, or Pockets the Kangaroo) who will be your teaching assistant and their friend. No student books are required!

Hands-On Bible Curriculum is also available for elementary grades.

BRING THE BIBLE TO LIFE FOR YOUR 1ST- THROUGH 6TH-GRADERS... WITH GROUP'S HANDS-ON BIBLE CURRICULUM™

Energize your kids with Active Learning!

Group's **Hands-On Bible Curriculum**™ will help you teach the Bible in a radical new way. It's based on active learning—the same teaching method Jesus used.

In each lesson, students will participate in exciting and memorable learning experiences using fascinating gadgets and gizmos. Your elementary students will discover biblical truths and <u>remember</u> what they learn because they're <u>doing</u> instead of just listening.

You'll save time and money too!

Simply follow the quick and easy instructions in the **Teacher Guide**. You'll get tons of material for an energy-packed 35- to 60- minute lesson. Plus, you'll SAVE BIG over other curriculum programs that require you to buy expensive separate student books—all student handouts in Group's **Hands-On Bible Curriculum** are photocopiable!

In addition to the easy-to-use **Teacher Guide**, you'll get all the essential teaching materials you need in a ready-to-use **Learning Lab**®. No more running from store to store hunting for lesson materials—all the active-learning tools you need to teach 13 exciting Bible lessons to any size class are provided for you in the **Learning Lab**.

Challenging topics each quarter keep your kids coming back!

Group's **Hands-On Bible Curriculum** covers topics that matter to your kids and teaches them the Bible with integrity. Switching topics every month keeps your 1st- through 6th-graders enthused and coming back for more. The full two-year program will help your kids make God-pleasing decisions...recognize their God-given potential...and seek to grow as Christians.

Take the boredom out of Sunday school, children's church, and midweek meetings for your elementary students. Make your job easier and more rewarding with no-fail lessons that are ready in a flash. Order Group's **Hands-On Bible Curriculum** for your 1st- through 6th-graders today. (Also available for Toddlers & 2s, Preschool, and Pre-K and K!)

Order today from your local Christian bookstore, or write: Group Publishing, P.O. Box 485, Loveland, CO 80539.